# PRAISE FOR THE 500 WORD WRITING BUDDY

"Alison Morton is the energetic and well-connected writer of a successful, ever-expanding series of alternate history thrillers and also of non-fiction, so advice on writing from her is always going to be worth reading. Her discipline as a writer is evidenced by her ability to encapsulate these nuggets of advice into neat and well-formed articles of just 500 words.

This little volume is a handy source of inspiration and motivation not only for the new writer, as the subtitle suggests, but also a tonic for writers at any stage who might be flagging or lapsing into bad habits.

As an established author myself, but always conscious of having more to learn and needing constant head-patting to keep me motivated, I thought this little book was a tonic and a pick-me-up that would benefit any writer. I'll be keeping it on my Kindle to dip into now and again whenever I feel the need of a cheerleader."

Debbie Young
Author of the Sophie Sayers Village Mysteries

# ABOUT THE AUTHOR

A 'Roman nut' since age 11, Alison explores via her award-winning Roma Nova adventure thrillers the 'what if' idea of a modern Roman society run by strong women.

Alison contributes to writing magazines and gives talks/workshops/panels on writing, self-publishing, alternative and historical fiction, research and social media at writers' conferences, tutorial groups and associations in the UK, US, Ireland and France.

She now lives in France with her husband, cultivates a Roman herb garden and drinks wine.

Find out more at alison-morton.com, follow her on Twitter @alison_morton and Facebook and sign up to Alison's newsletter (https://alison-morton.com/newsletter/)

# The 500 Word Writing Buddy

## 35 Inner Secrets for the New Writer

### Alison Morton

Pulcheria Press

Published in 2020 by Pulcheria Press
© 2015 -2020 Alison Morton
Propriété littéraire d'Alison Morton
All rights reserved Tous droits réservés

The right of Alison Morton to be identified as the author of this work has been asserted in accordance with the Copyright, Designs and Patents Acts 1988 Sections 77 and 78.

No part of this book may be reproduced, stored in a retrieval system or transmitted in any form or by any means, electronic, mechanical, photocopying, recording or otherwise, without prior written permission of the copyright holder, except for the use of brief quotations in a book review.

Tous droits de reproduction, d'adaptation et de traduction, intégrale ou partielle réservés pour tous pays. L'auteur ou l'éditeur est seul propriétaire des droits et responsable du contenu de ce livre.

Le Code de la propriété intellectuelle interdit les copies ou reproductions destinées à une utilisation collective. Toute représentation ou reproduction intégrale ou partielle faite par quelque procédé que ce soit, sans le consentement de l'auteur ou de ses ayant droit ou ayant cause, est illicite et constitue une contrefaçon, aux termes des articles L.335-2 et suivants du Code de la propriété intellectuelle

This book is a compilation of articles by the author and is not intended to be a comprehensive guide to all aspects of writing and publishing nor a replacement for legal or other expert advice.
The author accepts no liability or responsibility for any loss or damage caused or thought to be caused by using the information in this book.

ISBN 9791097310264

# FOREWORD TO THE FIRST EDITION
BY SARAH BERRY, FOUNDER OF THE DEUX-SÈVRES MAGAZINE

Our monthly magazine, created in 2011, reaches over 15,000 readers and is an invaluable resource to the department of Deux-Sèvres in South West France. Articles written by Alison and other local writers help the expat community hugely. Whether it is helpful writing tips, such as Alison's, or somebody sharing an experience, *The Deux-Sevres Monthly* helps somebody every day.

It's been a pleasure to have Alison writing for our magazine over the past few years. Her passion and zest for writing shine through in every article she produces and this has certainly helped guide our readers to begin, or continue, their writing whether it's an article, short story or that 'dream novel'.

I wish Alison huge success with her latest novel and future writing career.

Sarah Berry
Founding Editor, *The Deux-Sèvres Monthly* magazine

# INTRODUCTION TO THE SECOND EDITION

Under Sarah Berry's able management, *The Deux-Sèvres Monthly* became the acclaimed English language magazine it is today covering everything that could interest the English speaker living in rural France.

In 2011, I approached Sarah and offered her a column on writing and publishing. I wanted to pass on to other writers things I'd learnt since becoming a full-time writer. And our quiet corner of France was an ideal place to be creative!

The column was and is around 500 words; hence the title of this book. Each chapter is a 'quick 'n' dirty' introduction to each topic and intended to trigger further reading.

I've been delighted by the reaction to the first edition especially when writers come and chat to me at events. There is nothing like getting together with other 'scribblers'.

This edition (expanded from the original 25 chapters) covers five areas: writing your book; genres; you, the writer; publishing your book; and selling your book. Each section includes references for further reading and there is a useful contacts list at the back.

My thanks to editor Sarah for her support and to my critique partner Denise Barnes for her eagle-eyed checking.

**CONTENTS**

PART I
**WRITING YOUR BOOK**
1. The bones of your book                          3
2. Are you a pantser or a plotter?                 6
3. Doing your research                             8
4. Watching and noting                            11
5. New Year, new conflict                         14
6. A sense of time and place                      16
7. Full of character                              19
8. Style and tone                                 22
9. NaNoWriMo                                      25
10. You've written your novel. What next?         28
11. Preparing your manuscript for publication     31
12. "Oh, it's wonderful, darling!"                34
13. Editing – do I really need it?                37
14. Paid editing – do I really need it?           40
15. The next book                                 43

PART II
**GENRES**
16. Crime, mystery and thrillers                  49
17. Romantic stuff                                52
18. Speculative fiction                           55
19. Memoir                                        58
20. Historical fiction                            61
21. 'Women's fiction'                             64

PART III
**YOU, THE WRITER**
22. Why do you write?                             69
23. Something stopping you writing that book?     72
24. You don't want to be alone!                   75
25. Reading whilst writing                        78
26. Your writing space                            81

27. In the writer's head      84

PART IV
**PUBLISHING YOUR BOOK**
28. The traditional publishing route      89
29. Self-publishing the DIY way      92
30. Self-publishing with expert help      96

PART V
**SELLING YOUR BOOK**
31. Pricing your book      101
32. Selling your book – the paper version      104
33. Selling your book – the ebook version      107
34. How to launch your book      111
35. How to sell more books – write more books!      114

Further Reading      117
Some useful web and blogsites      119

*Would you leave a review?*      121
*The Roma Nova thriller series*      123

# PART I

# WRITING YOUR BOOK

# 1
# THE BONES OF YOUR BOOK

Writing exciting scenes is thrilling. And once you have set up your characters, they start developing their own story lines. Your narrative is thundering along and your story is flying.

But… you the writer, your characters and the readers need to take a break. So how and what?

**A break within a chapter**

A line space gives a visual signal that the scene will end or change location/time/lead character. You can cut out the dull bits of life (getting from A to B, climbing the stairs, having a meal, doing the bins) and tell the story without dropping the pace. If you can link the end of one scene across the bridge of the break line to introduce the next scene, then that's good writing technique.

**New chapter**

Sagas, historical novels and space operas will generally have longer chapters than romance and thrillers. Mind you, Tom Clancy seems to break this rule, but he has a *lot* of scene breaks within his chapters. I keep my chapters short, generally 5 to 8 pages, approx. 2,000 to 3,200 words, depending on how the narrative is flowing. Breaking for a new chapter allows the writer to finish on a revelation/cliffhanger/surprise/danger point and then drop into the middle of an entirely separate scene in the next chapter which pushes the story forward. Again, adding a link where the same object, phrase, weather or location is at the beginning of the next chapter but in a different context can be used here to great effect.

I like starting a new chapter in the middle of a conversation and then revealing where we are and what's happening; this keeps the momentum up especially in a thriller. Having said that, sometimes the beginning of a new chapter is a perfect place to put a little background detail as long as it contributes to the story and isn't an info-dump.

**Parts**

If you have quite distinct parts of a story, then you can split the novel into different sections. These big separators are often used to cover intervening periods, or to show that one phase of a person's life has finished and they're moving on to something or somewhere else. Classically, parts are three, like acts in a play, but can be any number, though five or six is probably the maximum.


All breaks can be used in a story with two timelines or in the same one to switch between different characters' points of view, e.g. from the protagonist to antagonist, but it has to be done carefully or readers will lose patience and skip ahead to continue the tale they were enjoying.

## Prologues and epilogues

Think whether or not you really need these as they can appear like dangly bits with no definite purpose. Could the information in the prologue be dripped into the story instead? Sometimes a hint of a deep buried secret or an event much earlier period of time is fine in a short prologue if it would seem out of place elsewhere in the novel. And finally, could the epilogue be integrated into the last chapter or do you really need that last word?

## 2

## ARE YOU A PANTSER OR A PLOTTER?

Do you sit down at the keyboard and just write, a vague idea of the characters and their story swirling around in your head? Then you're a pantser who writes by the seat of your pants. Maybe you plan every scene and chapter in meticulous detail, paying careful attention to the rules of structure used by your genre. Undoubtedly, you're a plotter.

Well, I'm not entirely sure these extremes exist, in the same way that Elinor and Marianne Dashwood don't but are symbols for extremes of Sense and Sensibility. When I write, I usually start classically: a character who is suddenly faced with a terrible dilemma, but I only discover how she's going to resolve it once I start writing her story.

However, sensible hat back on, I do like to know the point she's going to reach at the end. The story has to have some definite purpose otherwise it becomes a soup of pure muddle. But if I don't have free rein to develop the story, let the characters spark off each other or encounter and deal with setbacks, then I don't enjoy the actual writing. There's no point in creating a story if you can't have fun doing it!

Drafting the fifth book in my Roma Nova series, I learnt how to resolve this dilemma. Yes, I was acquainted with the main character and I wanted to tell her story. But that was it. I needed to let her run around in my head a bit, to have some adventures, get into trouble, struggle to get out, land in more – you know the rest. More than anything, I had to get to know her, to find out what she wants, what was stopping her, what she had to do, or "Goal, Motivation, Conflict", as creative writing tutors call it.

**The 30-line method**

My solution is to write down 30 lines of plot – less an outline, more of a wireframe as I prefer the 3D analogy.

Line 1: The beginning – the inciting incident/kick-off
Line 2: Impact and realisation of that event/situation
Line 3: The plan to resolve it
Line 6: First enormous set-back (turning point 1)
Line 15: First glimmer of light (turning point 2)
Line 21: Gritting on in face of terrible odds and sacrifice (turning point 3)
Line 25: Despite developments, we might be getting there – the false dawn
Line 28: Catastrophe/black moment – do or die
Line 30: The end – the resolution and loose-end tying-up

I haven't put all the lines in, but you get the idea. It's not fixed but it gives you a skeleton which holds the whole thing together but which will become absorbed into the finished product and never be seen by the reader. Once you have these thirty lines and accept that you might have to change or omit some of the lines and substitute new ones, then you can release your inner pantser, and create and imagine to your heart's content.

# 3
# DOING YOUR RESEARCH

You'll be writing your story and you'll discover you need to find out whether DNA testing existed in the 1980s or when the Romans swapped from segmented armour to chain mail. Or did they? And when did people start using zips in clothes?

**What exactly is research?**

Research comes in many shapes and sizes, from seeking out a forensic pathologist and requesting an interview to spending hours searching through history books, contemporaneous accounts and academic articles on the Internet and in the library. Fiction writers are often distracted, going for the shiny bits, poking at one idea before dropping it and moving on to the next glittering thing. Sometimes they become experts in their chosen subject almost to academic level. However, if you're fascinated by your research area, it's likely that your passion will come through onto the page for the reader to enjoy.

**Research pitfalls**

The most difficult thing about research is knowing when to stop, to let it go, so that you can get on with your story. Known as 'research thrall' among writers, it a bit like Golum and the Ring. So set a time limit for each session as well as for the whole book writing project. I try to limit it to roughly a third of my writing time.

With their ability to check facts at a few clicks of the mouse, readers expect you to be accurate. But although detail is important, 90-95% of what you have dug up shouldn't end up in your book.

You don't want to be one of those writers who feels compelled to jam in every last detail about what kind of buttons that regiment wore on their jackets, how the corn was ground to go into the bread the heroine was eating, unless, of course, it's vital to the story.

It doesn't matter that you took 10 hours, 10 days or 10 years to learn all this stuff, the reader doesn't want an 'info dump' in the middle of an absorbing story.

**Drip, drip, drip…**

Drip-drip is the best way, leaving little flashes of colour, hints about atmosphere and setting, whispers of sounds woven into the action. Most readers understand a castle on a hill. Have your heroine dirty her skirt when crossing the muddy yard, tread carefully avoiding the horse-droppings, smell the harsh lye soap from the laundry women's tubs, step back when the lord rides through the stone gateway.

Bet you can see that castle courtyard…

If there are strange words or technical terms, use them carefully and explain without explaining.

> *'She turned her back to me and took her time running her fingers over the pommel and down the creamy wire-inlaid grip of a ceremonial pugio dagger in the open glass display cabinet. The grooved, waisted blade was flat and wide with razor-thin edges. It was twenty centimetres of meanness.' (PERFIDITAS)*

By adding 'ceremonial' and 'dagger' to *pugio* the reader then understands the Latin word. The detail gives us an idea of the almost ritualistic significance of the weapon and the character's reaction to it shows there is danger and a distinct threat.

So whether you're writing historic fiction, a space adventure or a coming of age in the Australian outback, your story needs to have strong elements of both good research and good writing.

## 4

## WATCHING AND NOTING

When a writer's not at their desk, i.e. living their normal life, they spend a lot of time looking at other people and things. And jotting down details in the writer's notebook they *always* carry with them. Not, you understand in a stalker-ish way, but to see how people do ordinary things. You'd be amazed how differently people unload their shopping trolley at the supermarket checkout, or how they get on a bus or act at a post office counter. And as for the queue itself, that's a rich, rich area.

In my story *PERFIDITAS*, my heroine observes:

> *'Most people were preoccupied with their daily lives – children, job, taxes, sex, cat – and didn't notice anybody or anything else. Unlike television cop shows would have you believe, trying to find useful witnesses was a nightmare: nobody saw anything because nobody was looking.'*

Busy with our mundane tasks, we don't take much notice of other people. Think about when you go supermarket shopping; you scan the shelves for the items you're looking for and can pass your next door neighbour or work colleague without registering their presence.

On the train, once they've found their seat, most people pull out their book or paper and settle down to ignore everybody else. But if you spot somebody looking, observing, actively watching the other passengers, there's a strong likelihood they're a writer. Or possibly a police officer.

**Writers need detail**

Voices, mannerisms, walks, tics and "tells" – the best source is other people. The obvious things that separate us from others are height, weight, hairstyle, glasses, types of clothes, the way we move. But it's scratching our necks, crossing knees and arms, fidgeting, jumping at a noise, fiddling with bag or briefcase contents, shaking a paper out, popping a can of drink, jabbing the keys on our mobiles, sucking hair, flexing fingers to examine nails, pushing spectacles up to the bridge of the nose that characterise us. And all these tiny gestures round characters out.

Practise analysing exactly how features are put together in a face. You usually only need one good glance at somebody. Then write it down in your notebook. It's surprisingly hard at first. Often it's small things like the distance between upper lip and nose, the angle of eyebrows, height of forehead, angle of eyes as well as the basic shapes of a face – oval, long square, circular. If you have a drawing friend, describe the person you've observed to them and see how the picture turns out!

**In conversation with…**

Next, there are the conversations that can be a gift for writing dialogue: the pretentious loudmouth on the phone, the quick-fire teenage minimal word conversations full of hidden meaning, a group of work colleagues shredding another absent one, a pair of genteel ladies discussing their latest purchases at John Lewis, managerial types talking about strategy for their company development or where their gîte in France is.

Hand on heart, I have heard all those conversations on the London to Hastings line. One was such a delicious conversation between two couples trying to outdo each other about the London shows they'd been to see that I wrote it down almost verbatim.

You must be unobtrusive and not go anywhere near invading people's privacy – that's obvious – but don't neglect the opportunities that are handed to you from everyday life for gathering great material for your book.

## 5

# NEW YEAR, NEW CONFLICT

First of all, *'bonne année'* to all readers, and best of luck with all your writing projects. This could be the year your work is published!

This month, we're down to practicalities. Virtually all fiction, in order to have some structure and to keep the reader glued to the page, is based on a conflict of some sort. Time-honoured structures include one or more of the following:

- Fantasy versus reality
- Man/woman/creature versus life
- Man/woman/creature versus man
- Man/woman/creature versus nature
- Man/woman/creature versus him/herself
- Man/woman/creature versus society
- Man/woman/creature versus God
- Country versus country
- Race versus race
- Person versus illness
- Fish out of water
- Coming of age
- Boy meets girl

- Boy meets boy
- Girl meets boy
- Girl meets girl
- God versus god
- Nature versus nature
- Magic versus person
- Person versus magic
- Religion versus politics
- Child versus adult
- Adult versus child
- Opinion versus opinion
- Religion versus science
- Science versus religion
- Teacher versus student
- Student versus teacher
- Two worlds collide

**Is that it?**

No, because as soon as the main character is on track to solve the problem before them, you should throw in another conflict. It doesn't have to be a "stop the terrorist blowing up the world" type of conflict; it could be an agonising choice of whether to go to an event or not, or lose somebody's friendship or love. The key is the intensity of the emotions and thoughts generated by the conflict and the possible outcomes.

If you're not sure of how that would play out, jot down notes about say, three or four possible outcomes. Which one will fit your overall plot? Readers enjoy the frisson of tension arising from the difficulty the main characters find themselves in and root for them when they try to find a way out. It's every writer's job to supply that conflict.

# 6

# A SENSE OF TIME AND PLACE

By the first page of a book, if not the first paragraph, a reader should know where and when they are. So how do writers do this?

## 1. Say where and when the scene takes place

It can be a few words, or a couple of sentences, but should be precise.

> *'It was a bright cold day in April, and the clocks were striking thirteen.'* (1984, George Orwell)

You know you're not in a standard place: clocks don't normally strike thirteen, and a sense of starkness comes with the cold day and the succinct, factual tone of the sentence.

## 2. Drip, don't dump

Next, weave in little reminders of place in throughout your text, but avoid heavy dollops of full description. If you can give a hint of how it touches a character, then so much the better!

> *'I found Dania, in her bar just off the Via Nova. I raised my brows at its new look: stylish indigo and silver decor, with beautiful glass and ceramic mosaics. She must have given in and taken professional advice this time.'* (*PERFIDITAS*, Alison Morton)

Here, you have the Latin road name, a venue, the owner's name, a short decoration description, the fact that it's changed, the protagonist's reaction to that change and a glimpse into the owner's character all in a couple of sentences.

## 3. Don't overdo measurements and facts

Readers want atmosphere and mood, not to know a journey takes $x$ hours at $y$ speed with an average of $z$ mph. Just a few details of how the place affects the character and action can convey a world of meaning.

> *'Nor did she want to see England. From hearsay, it was a cold, misty land filled with surly peasants and a dour aristocracy who viewed almost everyone from Poitou as soft, pampered and tainted with heresy.* (*The Greatest Knight*, Elizabeth Chadwick).

Without dates or lists of kings and queens, or measurement, we know we're in a feudal society with peasants, aristocrats and heresy, we have one country's view of another, complete with pre-judgements, and potential conflict, and know that we're in Poitou, an old name for the French region.

## 4. Write for all the senses

Drawing a picture in the reader's head is important, but bringing in smells, sounds and texture which will give a rounded and more vivid idea of the story's action.

> 'It was Baltic rain, from the north, cold and sea-scented, tangy with salt. For an instant, he was back twenty years, in the conning tower of a U-boat, slipping out of Wilhelmshaven, lights doused, into the darkness.' (*Fatherland*, Robert Harris)

Here the wet (touch), and salty (smell) rain brings back the protagonist's more straightforward time as a sailor (memory).

## 5. Make the place and the action work together

A character brings one kind of mood to the scene and what happens in the scene will bring another. Add in a sense of place and time and the scene comes to life in a natural way.

> 'The island lay directly ahead, and as the boat approached the great Venetian fortification which fronted the sea, she felt both the pull of its past and an overpowering sense of what it still meant in the present.' (*The Island*, Victoria Hislop)

Time and place are not just for Dr Who, but for everybody.

## 7

## FULL OF CHARACTER

Good stories rarely happen without a structured plot, but they never happen without strong characters. A plot gives the reader the main character's goal; the dire consequences if they don't succeed; the challenges the character has to overcome to achieve the goal; new threats that present themselves along the way that could cause the character to fail in his/her mission; the sacrifices that he/she has to make to overcome original and new problems; and the ultimate gains and losses at the resolution of the story.

But for me, all this vital stuff is still +

not as important as the story's characters.

Characters are the life-blood of a story as they reflect real people. If the main character wasn't pig-headed, wimpy, over kind, casual, ruthless, wise or persistently worried, they wouldn't make the decisions in the story that they do. Their environment and experiences make them who they are. But how does a writer bring characters to life and make them credible?

## Ask them questions

Here are a few to get started:

1. What is your character's name and do they like it?
2. When and where were they born?
3. What do they do for a living and are they happy in their job?
4. Is your character married/living with somebody and how do they feel about that relationship?
5. Where does your character live now and why are they there?
6. Are they content, integrated or lonely in the place where they live?
7. Do they have brothers and sisters and how do they get on with them?
8. What impact do/did the character's parents or guardians have on them?
9. How does/did your character get on with them?
10. Does your character have children and what's their relationship with them?
11. Describe a significant memory from your character's childhood

Now, although very useful as a first step, this could seem a little formulaic, so next think about which actor you'd like to play your main character.

Stick a picture of that actor on your wall above your desk. I look at mine every time I write but I don't describe every detail about her, just enough of a foundation for a reader to build their own idea on.

After all, that's the fun of reading!

## Deeper and deeper

And then interview them or write a character study. You'd be amazed what you find out. I analysed Aurelia here: https://alison-morton.com/2019/05/16/meet-aurelia-mitela-warrior-diplomat-spy/ Even I was surprised!

As the story unfolds, the character reveals herself/himself to the writer. I know it sounds funny, but well-written and rounded characters start taking on a life of their own and running the story. This is A Good Thing. By the end, the characters have evolved, learnt something, are deeply affected by the events in the story, and have developed and matured as people.

But the essential is that characters must engage us as readers. We need to share their joys, fears, pain and pleasure. We are there when they fall in love or fall over. Their joy of their team winning or their child performing in the school play (even as third mushroom), the frisson of fear they feel when facing an enemy with a gun, receiving a joyful letter or devastating email, must be genuine for us to invest our precious reading time.

# 8
# STYLE AND TONE

Along with plot, character, theme, and setting, style is one of the fundamental elements of fiction; it shows *how* something is written, as opposed to *what* is written. If the style is consistent with the content, readers find the writing coherent, flowing and a pleasure to read. So what are the essentials of style?

## Tone

This refers to the attitude that a story creates towards its subject matter. It can be formal, informal, intimate, solemn, comedic, serious, ironic, condescending, etc. If a character is passionate about something, the tone of the writing will become very excited. Tone can draw the reader into the story as if they were the protagonist's best friend, or make them cautious and respectful as if they were a scary teacher from the first day at school.

## Context

The meanings of words and phrases change in different contexts. A good technique is to see yourself in the setting you are describing and brainstorm words that convey vital elements of that setting. If your character walks alongside a river, think of the vegetation: tall trees, wildflowers, walkers, riders trotting along on horses. If the story is set in the past, you may be either the proud rider or the peasant scurrying out of the way.

## Diction

Closely tied with context is diction, the formal name for nailing the correct type of word. Writers will choose one particular word from a selection with similar meanings so that it fits in with their story. For instance, in a 1930s comedy of manners, the heroine may say 'jolly good', in the 1960s, 'right on' and the 1990s 'cool' for the same good thing. This is where playing with words becomes fun, but in nearly all cases, there is only one word that will be correct for that point in the story.

## Wordiness and tightness

'Concise and precise' is the key to good style; weeding out unnecessary words, using adjectives sparingly and adverbs rarely, letting the nouns and verbs do their work. While polysyllabic words, alliteration, and consonance can be used to create sentences that roll off the tongue, be careful not to fall into the trap of over-flowery prose. Short, staccato words can be used to break up the rhythm of a sentence.

Although useful now and again, it's surprising how many qualifiers (very, often, hopefully, practically, basically, really, mostly) can be deleted, e.g. 'Most people usually think that many cats are generally pretty cute,' is better as 'Most people think cats are cute.'

## Imagery

To draw pictures in the reader's mind means using descriptive language that evokes sensory experience; a touch, smell or taste, the memory of a feeling of sadness, silk or sand, the emotions a sight of somebody or something evokes. Imagery may be in many forms including metaphors and similes but be careful not to fall into the cliché trap.

## Punctuation

And finally, good punctuation helps a style to be fast-paced, or more measured, with dashes, question marks, commas, speech marks and semi-colons. But keep the exclamation marks to a minimum!

All this may seem technical and cold in relation to what is after all a creative expression, but however imaginative and profound your writing idea is and however beautifully you express it, good style techniques will support and strengthen it.

9
---

## NANOWRIMO

What? National Novel Writing Month takes place every year when thousands of wannabe writers set out to write a novel of at least 50,000 words between 1 and 30 November, an average of 1,666 per day. In 2018, over 450,000 participants worldwide, 53,000 'winners' reached the 50,000 word mark by 30 November.

Now, it can be exhilarating to achieve this. Writing that much text is a high physical achievement let alone a mental and emotional one. The NaNoWriMo organisation structures the whole project, instilling writer discipline, a sense of fun and community and buzz throughout the month.

However (*and you knew there was going to be a however...*), 50,000 words of text does not a novel make. Most agents, publishers and readers consider 65-70,000 words as a minimum; 50,000 is a short-change.

The other big point is that such fast writing will produce a first draft and not a finished novel. Like tea, a manuscript needs to brew. Any professional writer will tell you that the first draft should go into the drawer for at least six weeks before you take it out and run the first self-edit. You'll be appalled at the mistakes, sloppy writing, plot holes and banalities you'll find – trust me.

Can you glue yourself to your keyboard and find 1,666 words every day, plus thinking time, plus research, plus real life? Some professional novelists write 500 words a day, some 3,000 a day or more. Some spend time on planning and research, others spend a year or more writing. Be advised that NaNoWriMo is not a guaranteed route to literary success.

**On the other hand…**

Let's look at the positive side. You're not trying to write the Great British Novel, you're trying to have a go at a story whose bones are good but which needs fleshing out and moulding. Put December aside, or more practically January to become NatEdRubbMo or "National Edit Your Rubbish Month." When you come back to it, the real work begins. If you want to do this novel writing thing, then you must come to terms with the fact that rewriting is an essential part of it. Writing is when you make the words. Editing is when you make the novel.

So, if you take part, how do you get the best out of the experience?

- Aim for, but don't despair if you don't reach the 50,000 mark. Know that you will have to work for several months afterwards on any text you produce
- Interact with others in the groups on NaNoWriMo – you may make some wonderful writing friends who will encourage you now and in the future
- If you get to the end of the month with a manuscript – finished or not – celebrate! Eat chocolate, drink a glass or two of bubbly, dance around the garden at midnight on 30 November

NaNoWriMo is seen by some as a gimmick. But that's not necessarily a bad thing. With an artificial month deadline and 50,000 word count, writing a novel becomes a challenge with a visible end-point that takes away a lot of the fear from the idea of *trying* to write a book. Writing becomes something achievable. As a gimmick, it's a pretty impressive one.

## 10

# YOU'VE WRITTEN YOUR NOVEL. WHAT NEXT?

Anybody who completes a novel, be it romance, thriller, historical, science-fiction, crime or adventure deserves a round of applause for the sheer hard work of writing it. Generally 70-100,000 words long, a novel takes at least four to six months to draft, another three to revise and a further three to polish. And that's if you're doing it full-time. Normal people have jobs, children, parents and lives so slog on for years, grabbing a few precious hours when they can. So congratulations!

**Next steps**

But now you've completed your manuscript, what are you going to do with it? Not everybody wants to publish. Some writers take enjoyment from the process of constructing and writing a story, others write it for family and friends. But many have a desire to see it in print and these days, digital form. It's the most thrilling feeling in the world to hold a copy of the book you've written in your hands.

Today, we're lucky to have many choices: print, e-book, formal publication through an agent and publisher, DIY or self-publishing, assisted publishing and partnership publishing. And hybrid and co-operative publishing are new kids walking onto the block along with audio.

## The traditional route

Traditionally, a writer polishes up their book, runs it past members of their writing group, or association and asks a fellow author to critique it. Sometimes, they even get it professionally copy edited. Next, they submit the final version to a literary agent to request representation. If the agent takes a writer on, they start the job of finding a publisher, and then handle all business arrangements including rights and royalties and negotiating contracts and overseas deals.

The writer then divides their time between working on the book with an in-house editor, publicity and promotion for that book and writing the next one, but mostly writing as they now have a formal deadline for that next book.

## Going independent

As it becomes increasingly harder to be accepted by an agent, and with publishers no longer accepting fiction direct from authors, writers are seeking other ways to publication. Some choose the full DIY route: paperback copies printed via Amazon's KDP Print, Ingram Spark or other POD (Print On Demand) companies plus an e-book version uploaded direct on to Amazon for Kindle readers and Smashwords, Draft2Digital or other aggregator for Apple, Barnes & Noble Nook, Kobo, etc.

Authors and publishers retain full control over how their works are published, sampled, priced and sold. If an author wants to give it away for free, they have that choice. But it's up to the author to organise formatting their book, designing a cover and acquiring an ISBN number so their book can be distributed through retail channels. I recommend reading Joanna Penn's *Successful Self-Publishing*.

## The must-dos

Two things are indispensable to make your self-published book of the same high standard as a traditionally-published book, or better: firstly, commissioning a structural editor who will look at the content, style and narrative development and then a copy editor who will correct and proof-read it; secondly, having a professionally-designed cover. Graphic designers who specialise in book covers, along with editors, are taking on much more work from independent/self-publishers as the sector grows.

Author service companies can provide a range of support from simple proofreading though to managed publication and book marketing. Some are excellent, but there are a lot of cowboys out there on the publishing frontier, so I recommend you read *The Independent Publishing Magazine* online at http://www.theindependentpublishingmagazine.com which lists and reviews the good, the bad and the really too horrible to describe.

## 11

## PREPARING YOUR MANUSCRIPT FOR PUBLICATION

You sit back, your mammoth writing task over. You've clicked Save, you've emailed your manuscript to yourself in case your computer dies (and/or saved it to Dropbox or the cloud), and you've reached for that well-deserved cuppa or glass of wine.

Ideally, you should put the novel away in a drawer, real or digital, for at least a couple of months. This gives you distance from the world you've been immersed in for the past few months. All professional writers admit their first drafts are rough. So when you can no longer resist the urge to work on your novel again, it's time for the red pen.

This is when you weed out the over-writing, the bad grammar, the poor syntax, unnecessary characters and those excessive adverbs and adjectives. And double-check any plot holes.

I like the red pen. Some say it's crushing, demeaning, aggressive. I find it's clear – an excellent contrast to black type on white paper. And, yes, you do need to print out your novel for this stage, in double spacing, so that you can write notes above and below the line.

I urge you to be strict with your own work, to try to detach and pretend it's another person's work, and that the other person has told you to spare nothing. You are not attacking your baby. Like a child, it needs both loving discipline as well as encouragement if it's going to grow into an independent, well-adjusted member of the book-world.

**How to start self-editing**

Make a cup of tea or coffee and sit in a quiet place.

1. Check you have indented each paragraph, except the first one in each chapter – indents or tabs, please, *not* spaces. No line spaces between paragraphs unless cutting to a different scene and then start the first line of the new scene with no indent.
2. Go back and do the research for technical points. If you have a climbing scene, do you know the difference between a carabiner and a belayer? Is your action hero using a Sig Sauer or a Glock? Does your heroine shop at the correct store in the correct street?
3. Check that eye and hair colours, and height and build of your characters are consistent.
4. Make sure a character doesn't know something before they've been told/found it out.
5. Make sure it's not snowing in June in the northern hemisphere or you have any eleven-month pregnancies.
6. Fill in, yes *add*, description/ narrative where you skimmed over it and where it's necessary. Make sure you've used all five senses, not just sight and sound. Half a dozen words or a simple sentence can bring a dull scene alive.
7. Check the voice is consistent and characters use the correct type of speech for their background and age.

8. Substitute 'dynamic' verbs for boring or limp-wristed ones and active voice for lurking passives.
9. Make every 'very', 'then', 'suddenly', 'mostly', 'quite', 'nearly', etc. justify its existence. They're usually not necessary.
10. Make every sentence a true gem – no clunkiness, no gratuitous or padding words. Is each word or sentence is necessary to the text?
11. Make your eyes bleed by checking that every single comma, semi-colon, colon, speech mark, exclamation and question mark is necessary, in the right place and correctly typed. And resist using exclamation marks!
12. Read the whole piece aloud.

And finally, repeat 1 to 12.

## 12

## "OH, IT'S WONDERFUL, DARLING!"

Really? You've written your piece (article, blog post, short story, novel, memoir). Defeating the inner worm hissing "Rubbish" inside your head and sapping your confidence, you've polished your work until it gleams. You've absorbed every article and book about self-editing, you've checked grammar, punctuation, structure and syntax until your eyes have nearly dropped out.

Then you've asked people to comment. That took guts, believe me, so congratulations for having done it. But all they've said is "I really liked it" or "I read it to the end" or "Aren't you clever!". They nod politely and you are stuck without a clue about what they really thought.

**What is feedback?**

For a writer, it should mean constructive comments given by somebody who knows what they're talking about with the aim of helping the writer improve. Honesty should be the core of this feedback.

Typical feedback providers range from friend, writing group, beta readers, critique partner, published author, professional editor. But bear in mind that as humans, we are risk averse, and would rather sell our grandmother into slavery than tell a writing colleague they have adverb diarrhoea.

## How to find good feedback providers

- Define your goals – do you want a general assessment, structural comments on narrative and form, or a detailed analysis with annotations?
- Who is doing it? What are their qualifications and experience? Do they know your genre?
- Define how you want that feedback given – verbal or written, in public or in private? Verbal gives you an immediate chance to respond, but written gives you the ability to go back and study it in detail.
- Think about what you can take emotionally and psychologically. Every writer, however successful, gets negative feedback and needs to be able to deal with it.
- Ask around, check online, find another writer in your genre. Build a relationship with that person so you can trust them to give positive and negative criticism honestly.

## Receiving and using feedback

- Be aware it takes time to read, assess and critique a piece of work properly, so respect the feedback-giver's work.
- Try not to react immediately or cry behind the sofa.

We want to be told we're brilliant, but 'it ain't necessarily so'.
- Many reports only mention places where work is needed, so they seem more negative than positive. Take 'grandstanding' and literary theory with a pinch of salt, but check they are not making a vital point in there.
- Disagreeing – your privilege. But think hard about why they've made a point you disagree with. Once you are sure, discard their recommendation with confidence.
- Finally, go through the report and mark up places to work on. This gives you an action plan.

**Giving feedback**

- Be very careful – this is not about you, but for the other writer. Make sure you are competent in the field.
- Organise your comments under headings so it doesn't turn into a meandering burble.
- Give praise where due but don't ignore the weak points of the text you're looking at.
- Be specific – why is it weak or strong? And quote examples. This will show the 'feedbackee' exactly where further work is needed.
- Offer alternatives and ways forward.

Good feedback is precious; no writer can progress without it. Take it on the chin and you may find your work will start to fly!

## 13

## EDITING – DO I REALLY NEED IT?

You've written your fabulous book and presumably, you've checked everything you can spot yourself. That first self-edit gets rid of the obvious horrors. But why should you use somebody else to edit it?

- Your readers deserve to get what they pay for – a top quality product.
- Your book needs to be in the best possible state to compete successfully, whether you send it out to agents or self-publish.
- You might be so close to your writing that you see what you know should be there, instead of what is actually there.
- Sometimes writers fall in love with their own work. They cannot see that parts of it are poorly written.
- A fresh eye looking over your work is likely to pick up on points that you may have missed.
- A professional, experienced editor knows what is acceptable for the market and will advise and guide you to get your work to publishable standard.

### So what are the choices?

In this article, I'll outline the less formal options; in the next, the paid professionals.

*Friends*

By all means ask friends to read your book. Every bit of feedback helps, and you should welcome it all. But beware: people are nervous of criticising their friend's work – they'd rather not offend. They will be in awe of the fact that you've written a book and may just say they loved it without saying anything useful to you as a writer. On the other hand, if they're a top fiction editor at a big publisher, seize their free offer!

*Writers' groups*

Creative writing groups provide a great forum in which to have your work critiqued by people as passionate about writing as you are. Some will be more informed and experienced than others, but there are bound to be people whose opinion you value. However, it's unlikely that someone in the group will offer to read and edit your whole novel unless you're prepared to do the same for them.

*Beta readers*

Non-professional readers who read widely and seem to love the idea of having a 'sneak preview'. They'll look through your manuscript and make suggestions to improve the story, its characters, or its setting. I use beta readers to see if my book is 'a good read' before the story goes for publishing.

• • •

*Critique partners*

A critique partner is gold. Usually writing a novel too, though not necessarily in the same genre, they will read the same scenes from your manuscript so many times that neither of you remember the count, and will give you completely honest feedback, however brutal. They'll discuss your characters' dilemmas and continually suggest solutions. Critique partners urge you to keep writing when you don't feel like it and won't let you give up. And you do exactly the same for them.

## However...

No matter how well versed your friends are in the rules of grammar, and the vagaries of the English language, only a professional editor is likely to handle dangling modifiers, tautologies, hyphenation of compound adjectives, repetition, consistency of punctuation, presentation of numerals, elision, etc.

In the next chapter, we'll have a look at the different kinds of paid editors; they all have a critical rôle to play.

## 14

## PAID EDITING – DO I REALLY NEED IT?

In the previous chapter, I outlined the 'free' editing possibilities – friends, writers' groups, beta readers and critique partners. Here, we look at paid editing help.

### Manuscript assessment/evaluation

Not strictly an edit, but if carried out by a competent, qualified person, it will be a more relevant and objective assessment of your work than anything you could get from beta readers, members of your writing group, your family or friends.

You may cry in the corner at first when you open it and/or pronounce it harsh or rubbish, but when you read the report again, point by point, you'll see the feedback and guidance are probably very honest.

Implementing the changes suggested will, almost without exception, help you tighten narrative, banish padding and produce a better book. Sometimes, it will help an author determine whether it makes sense to publish the book at all. Expect to pay £350-450.

## Structural editing

Sometimes called developmental or substantive editing, this is the most complex and time-consuming stage of the editorial process and also the most expensive (around £400-500). Many publishers are reluctant to take on books that need structural work.

A structural editor works with a manuscript as a whole and analyses how well its various parts contribute to the central message or narrative: plot, themes, structure, characterisation, pace, point of view, voice, dialogue, consistency and readability. They also look for a strong opening, good writing such as 'show don't tell', clear motivation, conflict, resolution and change for every character.

## Line editing

A line editor checks the quality of the prose, removes unnecessary repetition, restructures sentences and paragraphs so that they flow more smoothly together, and checks the subtleties of word usage. A good line editor can turn dull prose into something both engaging and seamless. However, this is more a process for inexperienced authors who have a story to tell, but are not used to writing. If you have polished your prose to make it attractive, clear, logical and well structured, you may be able to miss out this stage.

## Copy editing

A copy editor's job is to make the text 'clear, correct, concise, comprehensible, and consistent'. At this nitty-gritty level, they'll check grammar and syntax; ensure that singular pronouns represent singular nouns and plural pronouns, plural nouns; punctuation, whether to spell out numbers or leave them as numerals, capitalisation, Latin abbreviations, foreign words, quotations; how to use academic, civil and military titles; when to italicise words or use quotation and speech marks, etc. They will also check consistency of eye and hair colour, the layout of rooms, and characters' movements. Cost - around £400.

Believe me, *everybody* needs a copy editor. If you are on a budget, this is the stage *not* to miss.

## Proofreading

Often confused with copy editing, proofreading is the final check of the electronic file for minor mistakes in spelling, typography, punctuation, spacing, etc. before the manuscript is published. It's amazing how quickly the brain either skims or corrects mistakes automatically. You can proofread your own work only if have the eye of a velociraptor and can detach yourself from the text; beware of being drawn into the story.

## 15

# THE NEXT BOOK

You've written your book, edited it, sent it off to agent/publisher or published it yourself. It's selling online and in shops and the sales figures are growing steadily. You've been blogging and tweeting and writing guest posts to support your marketing. You're immersed in your book's world: you love your characters, you know the places they live intimately, you know what drives them.

Time to throw all that away, unless you're writing a series. Time to write the next book, or if you've started, to crack on with it. But just before you do, consider two things: fear of success and using lessons learnt.

**Fear of success**

If your first book was successful – good reviews, satisfactory sales, fame – you may hesitate to start tapping on the keyboard again. You're nervous to follow it up, nervous you can't write something as good, nervous of your readers' expectations. You worry you'll be revealed as a one-book wonder. This isn't quite writer's block, it's more a case of 'success block.'

You're more worried about whether your second novel will be acceptable or not than actually finishing it. You're more haunted by the success of your past work than focused on your current or future work.

Take heart. Most writers produce (and admit to) at least one duff book. Well, not duff, but one a little duller, less stylish, less enticing for the reader. But the next one may be a diamond. The more books you write, the better you get and the more likely you are to produce attractive and exciting books.

## Using lessons learnt

Writing a second book is different from the first in some ways and exactly the same in others. The most immediate lesson comes from comments, notes and amendments from the editor of your first book. I ran more checks for consistency in character behaviour and timeframes in my second book as a result.

My critique partner had checked the first book carefully for overwriting and so I was very aware of that particular danger when writing the second. And another plus – sometimes I had taken my editor's comments personally on the first manuscript, but this time I was much more objective. We were on the same team and had a common goal.

The other big advantage is that you know what the process is. However you're published, you know what's coming and can prepare in advance.

The positive side of the fear of success is that thanks to readers' willingness to write reviews you have an idea of what they like and want. Many were kind enough to discuss in detail what they liked about my first book, INCEPTIO, and what they would like different in future books. Gold dust for any author!

You have absolutely no idea if your second novel will be as unique, more resonant, or just downright better than the first. Will it sell more copies, touch more lives or get more stars on Amazon and Goodreads? But if it continues to exist only in your head, then you'll never know...

# PART II
## GENRES

## 16

# CRIME, MYSTERY AND THRILLERS

Crime, mystery and thriller fiction - is it a genre? Previously regarded as the poor relation of literary writing, these novels have been wildly popular from Conan Doyle to Stieg Larsson and Val McDermid, Erskine Childers to Ian Fleming and Robert Harris. Now, with writers like P D James, Ian Rankin and the late Ruth Rendell, nobody can doubt their quality.

So what do we mean by crime, mystery and thriller, or CMT for short? Whodunits and detective fiction are the classics, but all CMT stories give us excitement, fear, suspense, danger, and knowledge of body parts, state secrets and crazy people we would never normally experience.

## Crime fiction

Broadly, this term deals with crime, detection, criminals, and their motives. **Subgenres** include police procedural, legal thriller, CSI/forensic, courtroom drama and hard-boiled fiction. The protagonist can be the criminal, a police officer, an amateur detective, a female sleuth, but the story centres on finding out 'who', 'where' and hopefully 'why' after a crime is committed and bringing the perpetrator to account through the justice system.

Writing can be fast-paced, thoughtful and profound, or even 'slow and lazy', depending on the characters, setting and style. Readers increasingly love the technical side of crime writing, so research carefully!

**Thrillers**

These use suspense, tension, and excitement as their main elements and push readers' emotions to an intense level of anticipation, heightened expectation, uncertainty, surprise, anxiety and terror.

A thriller provides the sudden rush of excitement, and exhilaration that drives the narrative, sometimes subtly with peaks and lulls, sometimes at a constant, breakneck pace. It keeps the audience on the edge of their seats as the plot builds towards a climax. Red herrings, plot twists, and cliff-hangers abound.

Thrillers are usually driven by a villain which can be a physical person, an organisation/government, the setting, internal conflict, or just a revolutionary or mad axe person who throws obstacles in front of the protagonist but which the protagonist has to overcome to save the world, family, way of life or cat.

**Common subgenres** include psychological, historical, erotic, spy novels, comedy thrillers, romantic suspense, military, techno-thrillers, alternative history(!) and sci-fi thrillers. Writing in this genre tends to be succinct, gritty, rousing and fast-paced; the focus is on the plot. But woe betide a thriller writer who only produces cardboard characters.

People in thrillers may be cynics or innocents, special forces or ordinary people on the street thrown into a nerve-wracking situation, but their personal stories and backgrounds must be reflected in the narrative and affected by it.

## And mystery...

Who doesn't like an Agatha Christie or M C Beaton? Mystery fiction often involves a mysterious death, disappearance or an injustice to be remedied. In a closed circle of suspects, each suspect must have a credible motive and a reasonable opportunity for committing the crime. The central character is normally a detective like Poirot, who eventually solves the mystery by keen observation and logical deduction from facts neutrally presented to the reader.

Unlike hardboiled detective stories full of action and gritty realism, mystery fiction focuses on the puzzle or suspense element and its logical solution, and can sometimes involve a supernatural or paranormal element. Writing has to be precise and the plotting absolutely pinned-down or canny readers will spot any gaps or mistakes.

# 17
# ROMANTIC STUFF

February is firmly aligned with the heart's emotion and in the book world, romance is important. Romantic fiction authors can make a steady, occasionally spectacular, living as this genre sells consistently and well – romantic fiction amounts to an estimated 60% of all books bought.

Numerous more or less strict definitions abound but in general the twin requirements for romantic fiction are a focus on a developing romantic relationship and an optimistic ending – 'happy ever after' or at least 'happy for now'.

## Dishing the stereotype

The 'sweet young thing' waiting to be rescued (and possibly ravished in the best possible taste) doesn't cut it these days. Readers of contemporary romance like a more independent worldly-wise heroine who earns a living and takes on responsibilities of her own. Heroes are no longer universally masterful super-beings who know everything and can do everything while the heroine flutters her eyelashes.

Respecting the genre conventions is very important, but

writing needs to be fresh and original to succeed in a flourishing but competitive writing market.

Today, we see many sub-genres: paranormal, historic, fantasy, sci-fi, mystery and suspense and many 'heat' levels from sweet to erotic. A survey conducted by the Romance Writers of America found that nearly 50% of readers liked a side order of mystery with their romances. This can range from dark and edgy to cosy and light-hearted.

**Falling in love is not as easy as it used to be**

A romantic relationship can develop gradually or be the legendary *coup de foudre*. It can be tentative or intense – that's something that doesn't change – but readers like to see both hero and heroine change and mature during the story.

A heroine or hero who realises they are falling in love has two choices: to accept it and revel in it, or refuse it. This is the challenge today; people don't have to get married or become partners.

They may not only be torn between so many other choices, but also struggling with pressures falling on them. They may think of sacrificing their potential emotional satisfaction for their career, their cause, to pursue education, new experiences such as living overseas or just for their own self-respect if they doubt their love interest is trustworthy.

All excellent grist to the writing mill!

**Some key points:**

- A 'romance' focuses on the couple to the exclusion of everything and everybody else. Around 50-60,000 words, these are often shorter than the average novels.

- 'Romantic fiction' can embrace(!) other genres and include sub-plots and a number of secondary characters.
- 'Fiction with romantic elements' still keeps a relationship central, but other parts of the narrative may be more significant to the story.
- Well-rounded characters, not handsome/ beautiful cardboard cutouts, are essential. However, the hero and heroine do need to have a reasonable degree of attractiveness…
- Emotion and empathy are essential; despite Fifty Shades' success, raunchy sex alone isn't enough to sell books consistently. Several friends reported they became more interested in the characters' story than the, er, mechanical, side of the proceedings.
- Romantic fiction needs to express internal conflict and feelings around the main characters, but one that is resolved.

**Further useful information:**

The Romantic Novelists' Association http://www.rna-uk.org/
*Love Writing: How to make money writing romantic or erotic fiction*, by Sue Moorcroft (Accent Press)

## 18

# SPECULATIVE FICTION

Once upon a time, we knew what science-fiction was: Dan Dare, Flash Gordon, Jules Verne, War of the Worlds, Star Trek, Isaac Asimov, Dr Who – adventures in space and time. Then it branched out to include fantasy as 'SFF'– science fiction and fantasy.

Now it comes under a broad literary genre called 'speculative fiction' which brings together any fiction with supernatural, fantastical, or futuristic elements; utopian/dystopian tales, paranormal, alternate history, future history, horror, supernature, cyberpunk, magic and steampunk. The great Terry Pratchett leaps to mind, as do Margaret Attwood, Neil Gaiman, JRR Tolkein, George Orwell, George R R Martin and Robert Heinlein.

And nearly all books for children contains some aspect of speculative fiction, such as talking animals, magic, or monsters; two examples are the Narnia and Harry Potter series.

## Is it all just made up?

Fiction is by definition made-up; all of it involves some degree of speculation. But in 'speculative fiction' the author changes what's real or possible; the 'laws' of that world (explicit or implicit) are different from ours. As in other fiction genres, speculative fiction explores the human condition; it just chooses to do so in an imaginary setting.

You might argue that there's no need to ask what would happen if some people had magic powers, if there was a hidden world within our own, if we created robots and they rose up against us.

However, each of these scenarios says something about our human nature, our secret fears and desires, our social issues, our dependence on technology and tendency to abuse it, our competitive nature and willingness to explore every dark hole, no matter what monsters we may unearth.

## World building

A well-built world is the mainstay of speculative fiction. If you set your story in a different country, you can visit the places the characters would live in, smell the sea, touch the plants, walk under the hot blue sky, or freeze in a biting wind.

But if you invent that country, galaxy or dimension, you have to get your imagination going. Are there mountains, seas, deserts and rivers? How do people make their living? How are they educated? What kind of industry is there? Is the government representative? Are laws authoritarian or permissive? Who holds the power?

Believe me, fans will expect you to know everything from costume, social philosophy and weapons to food, transport and childcare provision. (*Yes, I was asked about that at the launch of my second book.*) You don't need to mention any of these as such, unless it impacts on the plot, but you need to have it all worked out in your head.

**Characters**

All the usual stuff about well-rounded, interesting, non-perfect characters applies, as does heaping trouble on them and making them grow and learn something from the story's conflict.

But in their world, the characters' experience of living in that place, and the struggle to make sense of it, is expressed through their culture and values, so their reactions, language and attitudes may be more robust or more flexible than those we expect. Sometimes this can be upsetting or even alienating to us, but true to the internal systems of your imagined world. But sometimes it can provoke us to think…

**Free writing guide**

A free guide to writing alternative history (a blend of history and science fiction) can be downloaded here: https://alison-mortonauthor.com/writing-books/writing-in-an-alternative-history-setting/ Much of it will apply to other speculative subgenres.

Why not try a little speculation in your own writing?

## 19

# MEMOIR

Most of us recognise an autobiography; it's the story of a life written by the subject, sometimes with a ghostwriter's assistance. Memoir is a story *from* life, an account of a particular episode or aspect of the author's life that has a theme, a universal idea that we can all understand, e.g. courage in the face of opposition, conflict between mercy and justice, a parent's loving sacrifice. Often it contains a powerful reflection on everyday life which can have lessons for us all.

Memoirs deal with childhood, travel, family, competitive sports, starting a company, turning points in family relationships, and today, a way of passing down a personal legacy. Sometimes, writing memoir gives a new perspective on the writer's own life, particularly eye-opening and even cathartic for the writer if there is a deep-seated issue fighting to be to be resolved.

## Being personal and vulnerable

Readers enjoy details that connect with them, whether heart-rending insights, daily trivia or small domestic objects. Good writers work their way into our hearts by being vulnerable, sharing the ugliest parts of their story, the parts any normal person would prefer to hide. Although they expose themselves, even embarrass themselves, they show their humanity. And that's what makes them so believable.

**Practical tips**

Some people have a burning story to tell; others may feel there is something bubbling under the surface which they can't quite identify. It may emerge naturally as they carry out a few writing exercises.

- Read other memoirs. You'll discover many different ways to approach point of view, style, tone, pace, chronology and more.
- Pick a theme for your memoir. Forgiveness? Justice? Redemption? Overcoming fear? Survival?
- Choose a scene in the story that's interesting, which drives the theme, and write that scene, sharing personal details but also universal truths. Aim for 250 – 550 words.
- Recall the first ever memory of doing X or feeling Y.
- Describe yourself at 5, 10 or 20 doing the theme even if you're not going to set the memoir at any of those times in your life – it fires the creative mind.
- Plot your life's six most significant moments: critical choices, influential people, conflicts, beliefs, lessons learnt, even mistakes. When you do it thoughtfully and honestly, one pivotal event will stand out as particularly intriguing and/or meaningful.
- Don't tell your story chronologically – start from the theme/impact/pivotal point.

**A few things to bear in mind...**

Writing is never neutral, completely fair or perfectly accurate. Writers debate long and hard about poetic licence and how far a non-fiction writer can go in crafting accounts of true events.

If you have kept a journal you will at least have a written record of what you thought on the day certain things happened. Interviewing other people who were there when the events happened can be critical; two or more sources dramatically improve the quality of the facts.

And lastly, you will be putting personal information out in public which may be about other people – think through the consequences.

## 20

# HISTORICAL FICTION

Ah, silk ball gowns, swishing of sabres, snarls of Roman centurions, scheming Plantagenets and toughing it out in colonial America... Who can resist escaping into the past?

Historical fiction can range from the soft, romantic and comedic through mystery, political, gritty and no-holds barred brutal to literary, learned and quasi-biographical. Whatever the style, the story should take place at least fifty years before the present, according to the Historical Novel Society.

**Consider these...**

Will your main character be a famous and documented real person or a fictitious one who may encounter them? The market is saturated with novels featuring the Tudors, but stories about minor or imaginary characters with less dazzling origins who touch on Henry's, Anne's or Elizabeth's lives can be just as mesmerising, e.g. C J Sansom's Shardlake series or Hilary Mantel's Wolf Hall series.

## Historical accuracy

The knotty question of historical accuracy spoiling a cracking tale is discussed on every historical fiction forum I know. We do not know the emphasis in conversations between people, let alone the content. People didn't document their lives in the way we do today on social media or our iPhones.

Conscientious authors who take small liberties such as changing a day, week or month of a battle will mention this as a note in the back of the book and give their reasons. This is *fiction*, after all.

However, gross inaccuracy such as marrying somebody to a different spouse, changing the victor of a battle or using materials or items not yet invented is unacceptable. Conn Iggulden, who wrote the meticulously researched Roman series about Julius Caesar (brilliant!) suggests that good historical fiction should fill gaps in the historical record *intelligently*.


## Oh, yes, the research

Research is a given: clothes, food, transport (especially timing), names, forms of address, housing, sanitation, weapons, medicine, farming, education, law, occupations, coinage…

But more important is immersing yourself into the mentality of the time. For example, from the 21$^{st}$ century we may wonder, sniff or scoff at how religion/beliefs ruled life in the past. How did intelligent Renaissance, Enlightenment or Roman people believe divine beings imbued their everyday life, how did nations split apart or slaughter others because of a wafer in a religious ceremony?

I recommend you read real accounts of lives at that time, identify and read experts' work on the period, then read some more. Spend time imagining how your $n$th century character would have carried out everyday tasks like opening the curtains. Did they have curtains, shutters or glass, or an open hole in the brick, stone or daub walls?

**Characters as people**

The key point is to remember that people are people, whether your story is of high politics, low cunning or battles and balls. To them, their life is natural and the norm; your characters shouldn't go around explaining their everyday life, so you will need to drip-drip the setting into the action of your writing.

And the realities of life – doing your duty, having enough to eat, protecting your family and friends as well as your back, telling tall tales to your mates, running a good home, showing off new clothes or goods, facing oppression, driving a bargain, joy or grief over a child, seeing marvels – none of this is new. And these are what will connect your characters in the past with the modern reader.

Find good historical fiction by fresh voices at Discovering Diamonds Reviews: https://discoveringdiamonds.blogspot.com
More at the Historical Novel Society – for readers *and* writers: https://historicalnovelsociety.org

## 21
## 'WOMEN'S FICTION'

I put this article's title in quotes on purpose because is a touchy subject.

'Women's fiction', now often called 'contemporary fiction' is considered an umbrella term for books focusing on women's life experience, and marketed to female readers. Its characters are often women attempting to overcome both personal and external adversity.

Although this fiction can deal with abuse, poverty, divorce, family breakdown or similar, it usually has a relationship at its centre. The resolution is almost always life-affirming, sometimes including romantic love, even if the story is a sad one.

Whether pure relationship stories, historical, generational sagas or mysteries, women's commercial fiction taps into the hopes, fears, dreams and even secret fantasies of today's woman. A man may be waiting for the heroine of these novels but he's not the centre of events. Stories of sisters or women's friendships, especially in college or a small community are currently very much in vogue.

## Does it sell?

Women are the majority buyers and majority writers of fiction for sale. Sophie Kinsella, Joanna Trollope and Maeve Binchy have been nominated or awarded prizes for warm, upbeat and emotional writing. Their combined sales are such that if all three were to lay down their pens simultaneously, British publishing would take a cataclysmic nosedive.

## But there are problems...

Women's fiction is causing some discussion in the literary world and particularly among women writers like Joanne Harris.

Firstly, 'women's fiction' is very broad, almost too broad; it can feature criminal acts, historical events, bubbly town life, gritty slums, shopping, depression, ethnic communities – you name it. It ranges from quite serious semi-literary novels through to mysteries and psychological suspense stories to real girly stuff, like the Shopaholic series, for example. Only the fact that a story is woman-centred and not obviously falling to any other primary category pushes it into women's fiction.

Secondly, the bigger problem facing 'women's fiction' (a term some consider patronising in itself) is that critics still don't take it seriously. It is still under-represented in the review sections of newspapers, discussions on the radio and the big prizes. The Women's Prize for Fiction (formerly Bailey's and Orange) is an honourable exception.

## Men's fiction and women's fiction – labels apart

If you publish direct on Amazon, you can pick a category from a long list that includes ten sub-genres of 'women's fiction', but none are labelled 'men's fiction'. A clear message; men are the norm, women are a sub-category. With the 'women's fiction' label applied to a book, is half the population in the world blocked off before the books hit the shelves?

Labels such as 'crime', 'historical', 'adventure', 'chicklit', 'thriller', etc. are used in the book trade to market books to readers and give guidance about the sort of book they think the reader would enjoy, but quite why books have to be gendered, goodness knows.

Spy thrillers, high seas adventures, coming of age during war stories and gritty Swedish noir are not labelled 'men's fiction', and given that women buy and read far more books than men, a good number of women must be reading all of these.

For me, a story is a story and should stand on its own merit whether it features a man or woman as its main character. Most fiction, after all, is just fiction: contemporary, general commercial fiction. A large chunk of that market will have a primarily female audience, but that doesn't mean you necessarily have to categorise it as women's fiction.

# PART III
# YOU, THE WRITER

## 22

# WHY DO YOU WRITE?

Ever thought about exactly why you write? This is not an airy-fairy question as it can affect what you produce in those hours at your desk.

Grab a piece of paper and a pen and write in one or two sentences your reason for writing. Just saying "I just have to" really isn't enough. If you know what you want from your writing, why you write, your writing will be tighter and more passionate and focused.

If you're not clear now, it will come back to haunt you later in your writing life especially when faced with choices which could mean pursuing one part of your goal but at the expense of neglecting another.

**Famous voices**

Some reasons I've heard from other writers:

**Ann Cleeves, Shetland series**

*I write to explore how I feel about the things that trouble me and to tell stories to entertain.*

. . .

### Adrian Magson, thriller writer

*I write because I must and it's what I've always wanted to do. Simple. I also work hard at it and believe it will come out right.*


### Liesel Schwarz, steampunk author

*I write because I don't really know how not to write. Making stories is something that is so intrinsically part of who and what I am, that I can hardly imagine what it would be like not to do it. Also, writing is a fabulous excuse to not do the dishes and the laundry.*


### Angus Donald, historical writer

*I write because I love to read; because I fell in love with the written word as a child and I'm still head-over-heels... I hope I'll be part of the reader-writer nexus long after I'm dead and that my words will give as much pleasure as I have taken from others.*


### Elizabeth Chadwick, historical writer

*I write because I have been telling myself stories of one sort or another almost from birth. It's a deep part of who I am.*


### Victoria Lamb, historical writer

*I write because it's my family business - and also because it's the best way I know to make a living.*


**Trisha Ashley, contemporary fiction writer** *I have perceived myself as being a writer from when I was a little girl and always had something I was burning to say. These days I just say it at more length.*

. . .

## Mari Hannah, crime writer

*I began writing in the mid nineties for practical reasons. I'd sustained a serious wrist injury that ended my career as a probation officer. For me, writing on a computer was physiotherapy following surgery but also to keep my mind occupied. I was bored at home and far too young to be retired. At the time I had no aspirations to become a professional crime writer. It was years when that thought occurred. These days, I write because I must.*

And the master, **Stephen King**... *I really can't imagine doing anything else and I can't imagine not doing what I do.*

And me?

The story was bursting to get out and was triggered by seeing a rubbishy film at the local multiplex.

'*I could do better than that,*' I whispered to my husband in the dark.

'*So why don't you?*' he replied.

And why I carry on? I just can't leave it alone...

## 23

# SOMETHING STOPPING YOU WRITING THAT BOOK?

What? Oh, yes. I just have to finish my coffee, load the dishwasher, clean the cat's bowl, check my Facebook page, nip on to Twitter – but only for five minutes – do the filing, have a Skype with my friend…

Even writing this article is a distraction. So why don't I settle down and do what I love and lose myself in my book's imaginary world for hours on end? This is a question that burns into every writer's consciousness.

**Facts:**

- Books will not write themselves; whatever fantasy you conjure up, the writing elves do not visit overnight
- Editors and agents get cheesed off with undisciplined writers
- Your fans repeatedly ask when your next book is out
- The only way to sell more books is to write more books

**Making time**

Even if it's only half an hour or an hour, everybody is entitled to some 'me time'. Be ruthless during that time – no Internet or other interruptions. I was cheered when a famous author admitted to me that she wrote one paragraph at a time, flitting back and forth to the computer for intense bursts of half an hour at a time in between doing a million other things. She dismissed the idea of x words per day with a wave of her hand. Yet her output is prolific.

**Lack of confidence**

Perhaps you ask yourself, *'Am I churning out rubbish or is there a possibility that somebody, somewhere will love my work?'* If you've had feedback through a writing group, a writers' organisation, a reputable on-line critique site, an agent/editor or published author, you can probably answer that question. And have some idea about what to improve on.

Even if you think your latest work is total rubbish, give yourself permission to write badly – you have the luxury of going back and fixing it by rewriting it. Again and again. And it will improve. And sometimes, doubt about your beauteous prose can make you look at it with a sharp eye. Perhaps you do need to change that character's story arc, or inject some emotional punch into that beige scene.

**Guilt**

Does the doubt about whether writing is a proper thing to do hammer away in the back of your brain? Many writers are prey to this one. Yes, it is a proper and fit occupation. How do you think all those books you love to read come to exist?

Many people can't string a sentence together. It's a great

skill, as is the gift of being able to weave a coherent story of tens of thousands of words that can make people's spirits soar, take them on an emotional journey, put them in the middle of a struggle for survival, or a famous battle of antiquity.

Like any other art form, it's difficult to make a living, but what is produced brings enormous pleasure individually to many and makes the world a far better place.

## 24

# YOU DON'T WANT TO BE ALONE!

Sitting by yourself, in a spare bedroom, study, or even at the dining room table, and tapping away can be a lonely business. People wonder why you don't go outdoors on a sunny day or wander into the village for a leisurely drink at the local bar or browse around the market. You don't want to see, let alone talk, to other people. You are absorbed in your writing world.

Of course, you need to get the word count or the hours in on your latest work – that's understood. But why do you need to interact with other people?

Ninety-six percent of people are not interested in writing or in your latest work, you mutter to yourself. You've often watched their eyes glaze over when you reply honestly to the enquiry about how your writing is going. But four per cent *are* interested and you need to find them.

### Why interact with other writers?

- Your mental health – you are a human being who needs contact with like-minded souls
- Learning from others' experiences – competitions,

agents, the ever-increasing number of routes to publication, conferences, writing and book events
- Getting critiques from other writers – not Auntie Maud who taught English or your mate at work, but working writers
- Learning new writing techniques and approaches to work – not just how to sling words together, but about characterisation, the senses, novel or poetry structure, research
- Networking to make those vital contacts to get your book published
- Not boring your nearest and dearest

So where are these fellow-writers? Starting locally, try to find a writing group. Look in the local press and on online in places like Facebook. Ask anybody who has a faint connection with writing. Ask at your local library and book club. Have a chat to the organiser and go and try out such a group. The main requirements are a supportive open atmosphere, honesty and a lack of ego-tripping!

Next are writing associations, usually specific to a genre of writing, such as the Romantic Novelists' Association or the Historical Novel Society. They have events, newsletters, Facebook pages, websites, blogs – you name it! ! If you are thinking of self-publishing nothing beats the camaraderie of the Alliance of Independent Authors (ALLi). Even remotely, you can benefit enormously.

**Taking the next step**

Online critique groups like can be a little daunting at first, but as you grow a writer's thick skin, you're likely to find it helpful and inspiring as well as immensely valuable. But you'll need to plunge in!

Going to conferences can be a real boost to your writing. There are hundreds of literary festivals each year in the UK, including more practical ones for writers which include workshops and masterclasses and events where you can meet fellow writers, agents and publishers.

Moreover, you may hook up with another writer you can develop into a writing buddy, or more formally, critique partner. With Skype and email it's no problem to discuss and work on writing together at distance. The writing buddy must be someone you trust, so it may take a little while to get to know them. Mine has kept me sane so they're worth their weight in gold! And she will have scrutinised this article before it goes for publication...

# 25

# READING WHILST WRITING

All writers should read. We all read what we want, what we love, and most writers I know read their friends' books, but are you reading your genre? Reading other books in your genre lets you know what the current writing trends are in your field, what's popular with readers, and what other writers are up to. But more importantly it's about staying current in your profession. A by-product is that you find new reading pleasures, discover new ideas and fresh insights.

**Getting a grounding**

Reading the classics in your genre will give you a grounding in how it's developed. Historical fiction for many, ahem, mature readers means Anya Seton's *Katherine*, Jean Plaidy's Tudor, Plantagenet and Borgia series, Robert Graves's *I, Claudius* or Nigel Tranter's Master of Gray series.

Now, Philippa Gregory, Simon Scarrow and Elizabeth Chadwick are the trendsetters with more detailed, gritty and psychological approaches. You have to know where your genre has been to know where it can go.

As I write alternate history thrillers with a Roman theme, I read Roman historical, spy and thriller novels as well as alternate history: William Boyd, Lee Child, John Le Carré, Diana Gabaldon (Outlander series), Lindsey Davies, Simon Scarrow, Conn Iggulden, Robert Harris (*Fatherland*, *Pompeii*), C J Sansom (*Dominion* and the Shardlake series), to name a few.

If you're approaching agents and publishers, they will want to know if you know how your book compares to others in your genre and how your book is different.

### Outside the covers

But, if you *only* read things within your category or genre, you run the risk of developing writer's blinkers. As your best friend might say if you stay in and do nothing but write, 'You need to get out more.'

So, if you spread your reading time, what are the benefits?

- **It will get you thinking in new ways, even inspire you.** In genre fiction such as thrillers, plots and characters tend to develop in roughly similar patterns. That's not to say each novel isn't unique in its way; it is. But reading a completely different author, such as Jane Austen or Isaac Asimov can make your brain work in a different way and spark your creativity.
- **You can discover ways to innovate and adapt your writing.** Reading outside your genre allows you to compare what you're reading to your own genre. You may find you consequently approach your genre from a different angle, see new possibilities, and find ways to personalise your fiction that other writers in the genre haven't thought about.
- **You can take a mental breather.** As much as I love alternate history, and I love writing my stories,

sometimes I feel inspiration ebbing and need to feed my brain with something different.
- **You have a mini-adventure.** Reading something that's new and different for you means embarking on a personal journey you've never taken before. In *The Road Back* by Liz Harris, I not only revisited the 1950s of my childhood, but learnt about Ladakh, northern India, as well as reading a beautifully written love story.

I read medieval, eighteenth century and Second World War historical fiction, modern adventure, romance, sci-fi, sagas, fantasy – you name it – and it always refreshes my writing brain.

## 26

# YOUR WRITING SPACE

Writing is deeply personal, as well as individual, so you need a place to work in that's comfortable, light and not subject to interruptions. Physical must-haves for the writing environment include a computer with appropriate software and Internet connection for research, a supportive chair and some bench, table or desk space for notes and reference books.

Yes, I still use some print books such as a complex thesaurus, style guides and a Latin grammar! But mostly, I use the Internet for dictionaries and basic thesaurus as the first place for looking things up. Obviously, when researching anything online, you have to be extra careful to assess the source of the information on the screen and cross-check everything, but it's quick and instant. For more profound or academic research, then it's the specialist libraries or even the British Library if all else fails.

**Where to write?**

Libraries can also be good places to write as long as you can get to one without too long a journey eating into your writing time and they have a quiet room. Many contemporary authors use coffee shops. Wherever it is, it's best not to have a window that looks out on to an interesting view – too distracting. Nor a nook under the stairs where everybody passes by with a cheery "How's it going?" every ten minutes.

Virginia Wolf maintained you had to have a room of your own to write in. Thomas Mann preferred writing in a wicker chair by the sea. Corinne Gerson wrote novels under the hair dryer in a hair salon. William Thackeray chose to write in hotel rooms. And Jack Kerouac wrote the novel *Doctor Sax* in a toilet in William Burroughs' apartment. JK Rowling wrote her first Harry Potter in cafés.

Ernest Hemingway said simply, "*The best place to write is in your head.*"

**How to write in that place**

You'll probably find it easier to establish a regular writing schedule if you can write during your most energetic time of day. Some writers get up an hour before the rest of the family does so they have a quiet time.

The advantage of morning writing is that you are fresh from the night's sleep. Also, once you've written the number of words you promised yourself to write, you're free from guilt about procrastinating all day. Not everyone's body clock is the same, of course. You may prefer to write in the evening; up to you to gauge when you can produce meaningful work.

When circumstances prevent you from writing at your best time of day, however, don't use this as an excuse not to write at all. Even twenty minutes of free-writing at your worst time of day is better than no writing. And writing daily keeps you in the habit.

## The frenemy Internet

I mentioned a connection to the Internet earlier. This gives you access to the world's knowledge, but while emailing people and talking on Facebook and Twitter can be fun, you need to ensure that you're not chatting and surfing online at the expense of your writing.

As you probably know, messing around on the Internet can be absorbing. But it's the biggest time-suck known and if you're not disciplined you can forget to get on with the writing. Allocate a specific time for online activity. Enjoy it then close browser and email until you have done your writing.

## 27

# IN THE WRITER'S HEAD

What really goes on in the head of that person hunched over a computer grunting and tapping away at their latest masterpiece? Are they dreaming up new plots, imagining engaging or repelling new characters, working fiendish traps into the narrative?

Could they be tasting the salt air as they surf the Californian waves, freezing their extremities off as they hack up the Alps behind Hannibal's elephants or half-dozing as their water-taxi drifts through warm lagoons? Or maybe they're just fantasising about chocolate or the latest car on Top Gear.

Probably some or none of this.

### In my own head

My first set of characters had been living in my head for years before I started to write my books. Although I have a general outline of each plot, the detail tends to evolve as I go along. Sometimes, the characters push to take over the story, but I have a little talk to them in my head, we agree on a compromise and I nudge them back into the story.

When I develop them, I go into distracted mode. Travelling anywhere as a passenger is perfect – plenty of hanging around time in airport lounges and waiting rooms when I can work out scenes in my head. But I have to be careful to keep it in my head; a very concerned face came into view once in Poitiers airport with an enquiry about whether I was alright? I'd been imagining a conversation, well, an argument, between my protagonist and her partner and I'd started speaking their lines out loud...

### Dealing with the rest of the world

In Real Life, writers can keep up quite a good act giving the impression they are paying attention. It's only when you find six trays of special offer pork in your supermarket trolley and no milk you realise you lost concentration again and had slipped back into the imaginary world...

Writers become obsessed about words and can become irrational at the sight (please, not 'site'!) of the grocer's apostrophe for plurals, 'less' instead of 'fewer' and 'your' instead of 'you're'. Their mouths pucker as if they've eaten too many Twiglets, their eyes narrow and all around should brace for a grammar lesson.

### No pressure?

Today's publishing world provides additional pressure – the constant need to be doing; writing, blogging, editing, research, promoting, reviewing. Which of these takes priority? We all know the answer should be writing, but if potential readers don't know about the book, it won't get read. Unless the writer visits other blogs, tweets, posts on Facebook, gives talks and public signings nobody will know.

So the poor writer dithers about which to do next and ends

up totally distracted, hands grasping his or her head and emitting a silent scream.

But the very worst are the twin horrors that buzz around in any writer's head. Firstly, a lack of confidence in their work *'Am I churning out rubbish or is there a possibility that somebody, somewhere will love my work?'* Secondly, guilt about whether writing is a proper job or frittering of precious time.

So next time you spot a writer mumbling to him or herself, looking enraptured or depressed, or ticking on about adverbs or apostrophes, give them a bit of slack.

# PART IV

# PUBLISHING YOUR BOOK

## 28

# THE TRADITIONAL PUBLISHING ROUTE

Although there are many pathways open to you (mainstream, self-publishing, assisted publishing) the usual way up until now has been the author-to-agent-to-publisher-to-bookseller route.

Finding a literary agent to suit you is not easy; even if they are willing to take you on, you have to be sure they are the right person to negotiate for you, sell your rights to best advantage, promote your career and look after your interests and sometimes your sanity.

If you write romance, you need an agent who knows the romance publishing houses; ditto for crime and thrillers, sci-fi or historical fiction. You can find all this information in the *Writers' & Artists' Yearbook* (WAYB), a weighty tome, but worth that weight in gold and saved postage. Thankfully it's now available online for a subscription: https://www.writersandartists.co.uk

### Sending your work to an agent – the nitty-gritty

So, having drawn up a list of appropriate agents from your research and checked out the *exact* submission guidelines on their websites, you can start putting a submission package together. This is usually a covering letter, a one-page synopsis of your novel and the first three chapters or fifty pages. Sometimes they ask you to email the whole book.

However, many agents are now following US practice and ask you to send a query letter or email first, outlining your book idea. This enables agents to see what your writing looks like as well as assess whether your story has commercial legs.

Each agent is different and I cannot stress strongly enough that you should adapt your materials (letter, synopsis, chapters) to comply with what they ask you to send. Don't send anything less or, worse, more. Nor any presents, weird fonts or fancy poems – they hate it.

The covering letter should be a simple introduction to your novel, including word count, genre (crime, romance, historical, etc.), a couple of sentences about the book and two more about you. You should end it with how you see it fitting into the market and sign off with a polite 'Thank you for your time.'

**The dreaded synopsis**

Writing a synopsis tends to strike Zeus' lightning bolts of fear into writers' hearts, but it needn't. It's a page outlining the action in the book, tells the agent briefly about the characters, their motivation and goals. You then describe the main crunch points and the final outcome. The agent wants to see if you know how to tell a convincing story and can imagine characters gripping enough to interest the reading public.

The WAYB gives good, solid advice, but I'd also recommend the following two ebooks for their invaluable practical help: *Write a Great Synopsis* and *Dear Agent: Write the Letter That Sells Your Book*, both by Nicola Morgan, Crabbit Publishing, 2012. She also produced the excellent *Write to be*

*Published*, published in paperback by Snowbooks, 2011 *(No, I'm not on commission!).*

## Other opportunities

Sadly, very few publishers and certainly not the big houses accept unagented manuscripts. Some local, specialised and independent presses will, though. You can find them at https://www.ipgbook.com/publishers-pages-32.php
Approach them in the same way as agents.


Finally, if you have a birthday coming up here are a few suggestions for book presents your nearest and dearest could buy for you, or perhaps you could treat yourself.

*Self Editing for Fiction Writers*, Renni Browne & Dave King, Collins, 2nd ed., 2004
*Bestseller*, Celia Brayfield, Fourth Estate, 1996
*Wannabe a Writer We've Heard Of?* Jane Wenham-Jones, Accent Press, 2012
*On Writing*, Stephen King, NEL, 2001

## 29

## SELF-PUBLISHING THE DIY WAY

In the previous article, I outlined the traditional route to getting your book published. The other end of the spectrum is DIY self-publishing.

**The pros of self-publishing**

- Keeping all the profits after any expenses such as cover design and editing
- Control over when to publish, cover design, book design and layout, pricing
- Ability to upload the eBook version very quickly
- Most importantly, **retaining all the rights**. These rights include different formats (large print, audio, paperback); media (film, television, radio); translation versions, etc. and can become a substantial part of an author's income.
- Being part of the cutting edge of book publishing at the most exciting time in its history

## The cons of self-publishing

- Tracking down a good editor and skilled cover designer – both essential for a quality book
- Learning to format and typeset
- Educating yourself about electronic and physical book distributors
- Learning about ISBNs, registrations, Nielsen listing
- Getting your print version stocked in bookshops
- Running your own marketing campaign
- Dealing with the prejudice against the self-published book, although that has faded significantly. Many trad published authors are now also self-publishing.

## Some facts about self-publishing

- The groundbreaking Taleist survey of 1,007 self-published authors found the average yearly earning in 2011 was $10,000
- Half of writers earned less than $500
- Romance writers earned 170% more than in other genres
- The worst earners were science fiction and literary writers
- The highest earners wrote over 2,000 words a day
- Self-publishers who received help with story editing, copy editing and proofreading made 13% more than the average
- Help with cover design increased earnings by 34%

**Some hard questions to ask yourself**

- Do you have a novel you believe in?
- Have you had somebody else other than friends and family cast a critical eye over it?
- Are you willing to invest financial resources into editing and cover design?
- Are you willing to invest a huge amount of time and energy to promote on social and other media?
- Are you prepared to educate yourself about the industry and interact with other authors, either online or in a writers' group?
- Are you looking at self-publishing as part of a career plan, and not just a get-rich-quick scheme or because of frustration?

**Where do you start?**

When you are sure you have polished your book, you need to think whether you want to publish just as an eBook – now the most popular way to publish a novel – or as a printed book, or both.

Next, I recommend visiting Smashwords, the ebook distributor (www.smashwords.com) which offers free downloadable guides, Draft To Digital (https://www.draft2digital.com) and Amazon (kdp.amazon.com) which gives you a mountain of information.

Best of all is the Alliance of Independent Author (ALLi)'s resource centre (https://selfpublishingadvice.org/alli-blog/). Everything is there!

For a printed book, one of the most popular choices these days for an DIY self-publisher is Amazon's KDP Print (https://kdp.amazon.com/en_US/) or Ingram Spark (https://www.ingramspark.com), part of Lightning Source which produces the world's books.

These companies produce Print On Demand (POD) books which means your book is only printed and shipped when a customer orders it. Although a little more expensive per book than a full print run, you avoid a garage-full of books wilting in the damp.

### All a bit much?

But if full DIY is a bit daunting, you could buy in specialist publishing services, either piecemeal or in a package. But that's for the next article…

## 30

# SELF-PUBLISHING WITH EXPERT HELP

Looking at DIY publishing in the previous chapter, I touched on some of the tasks: full copy edit and proofread; formatting and typesetting; professional cover; designing the interior; ISBNs, registrations; getting a print version stocked in bookshops; uploading the ebook to the various platforms (Kindle, Nook, Apple, Kobo), elbook and physical book distribution; running your own marketing and sales campaign.

If you don't want to take that lot on board, there is another way. The book marketplace is fiercely competitive. Very few writers, even established ones, have all the talents to publish their book without outside help. The absolute minimum recommended by successful self-publishers is a professional edit and a well-designed cover. Using an expert for these two will bump your sales up a few notches, but then there's all the other stuff.

## Using professional help

Paying a publishing consultant or a reputable publishing services provider (PSP) is like recruiting an invaluable ally. The author pays the PSP for its services to publish the book in a similar way that a traditional publisher does. But instead of the publisher buying all the rights to an author's work and paying a 7-10% royalty on sales after being reimbursed for any advance payment to the author, the author retains all his or her rights and profits.

Good PSPs will offer a range of packages from the straightforward or economy package to a full tailored service. Many offer single services such as editing if you don't want to have a complete package.

**\*Rights alert\***

The author is shown at all times as the copyright holder. This is **extremely important**. If you are paying somebody else to do the donkeywork for you, on no account should you cede any rights in any agreement you sign. The only thing you are granting the PSP is a **non-exclusive** licence to publish your book. Anything else is a rights grab and compromises your position.

Using a PSP is **not** vanity publishing. Vanity publishers will take anything, however badly written, as long as you are willing to pay. After production, print and submission to online booksellers, anything more is an additional paid add-on, even the production of the essential e-book.

There are good PSPs and there are not so good PSPs. The professional ones act like traditional publishers in that they won't accept every author who comes to them waving a manuscript. As a filter, good PSPs stipulate a full manuscript assessment before providing a quotation.

**How to find a good company**

Ask other authors and consult sites like the online and excellent *The Independent Publishing Magazine* (http://www.theindependentpublishingmagazine.com/) which scores and scrutinises all types of self and independent publishing support. Join the Alliance of Independent Author (ALLi) (https://selfpublishingadvice.org) and benefit from their watchdog service as well as all their accumulated wisdom.

Research books published by these providers: feel the quality of the paper, is the text tiny or squashed on to the page with no margins? Does the cover scream 'amateur' or is it well-designed? Can you read the back cover blurb? Are the front cover fonts clear and easy to read?

Signs of a good PSP:

- Taking time to listen to you, to hear about your work and discuss your target market
- The offer of a full range of professional services delivered by qualified and experienced staff
- Proven track record of commercially viable books
- A clear quotation
- Willingness to put you in contact with existing clients
- A website that is book-oriented, not services oriented

**The half and half solution**

If you decide to project manage the publication of your book yourself and select individual providers for cover, editing and so on, the same method and many of the same criteria in the previous paragraphs apply.

Assembling a team of experts takes time, but is well worth it to make your book the best it can be.

# PART V

# SELLING YOUR BOOK

## 31

# PRICING YOUR BOOK

Today, publishing a book yourself is fun as well as hard work. But if you are going to sell rather than give your book away, then you need to think about the selling price before your book is ready to release. Consider the book's potential audience and what you hope to accomplish with the book. Are you looking for readers or sales? While most authors would probably say both, when it comes to pricing strategy, it's best to focus on one and let the other follow.

Sadly, there is no secret formula. Every book is different. Every author is different. Every reader is different. Whether you're working on your first book or your twentieth, consider these four things.

### 1. Put the reader first

You've spent a lot of time working on your book. If you've hired professional editors and designers, you've also spent some money. But think about people who know nothing about your work. To them, your book is just one of hundreds of similar books. So instead of starting from 'what is my book worth?', ask 'what are readers willing to pay for THIS book?

Do they know my writing, or are they taking a risk on an unknown writer and their work? Are they going to get fair recompense for their reading hours invested?'

## 2. Consider your status

For unknown authors, a lower price can attract readers who are willing to take a chance on competitively priced ebook, say 99 or 1.99. However, authors with an established fan base from previous work, or a good social media platform, can charge more for their work. You may think it a good strategy to set a low price for your first book and/or for, say, the first three months or even a year, in order to become well known and thus increase your fan base for your second book.

## 3. Consider your genre

Focus on books from your own genre when comparing prices to get the most accurate picture of the market. If you write in a genre where people buy frequently and read quickly, such as romance or crime, a low price can make a big difference to a buyer's ability to buy more. For literary fiction or nonfiction your readers may buy less frequently and have different price expectations.

Whatever strategy you decide, I suggest not exceeding £5/$6 for a fiction ebook. Test out different price points with short-term promotions. Retailers like Amazon pay higher royalties for ebooks priced between £2.99 and £9.99.

## 4. Print books are different beasts

Publishing a print book means there is a manufacturing cost for that physical product. This base price, plus the slice the retailer deducts, is the minimum amount you can charge the buying public. However, you'll wish to add a markup that enables you to at least cover your expenses and make a small profit. And you should leave a little margin that allows you to give a small discount on special occasions.

Print books are often not viable as such, but they make excellent gifts and there is nothing quite so lovely as the feel of a solid book in your hands. On a practical front, they are excellent marketing tools and support your credibility as an author of 'real' books. And of course, you can sign and sell them at events as a lovely souvenir of the event for the reader.

## 32

# SELLING YOUR BOOK – THE PAPER VERSION

One of the areas where boundaries between traditional, DIY and assisted self-publishing are dissolving is that of marketing and selling books. Unless you are already a famous author, a star chef or 'off the telly', traditional companies are unlikely to spare budget for more than a six-week publicity push.

If you are represented by an agent, a good one will support opportunities for you, but the majority of authors have to muck in and market their own books. Some publishers run joint blogs to which all their authors contribute, but many don't have the resources or time.

If you self-publish, you are definitely the one who does the work!

## How print books are sold

*Traditionally published books* are sold into bookshops as part of the publishing deal. Nothing sells books like physical shelf presence. And your book could be in hundreds of outlets. But even the bigger shops can only stock 100,000 titles and well over 200,000 are published annually.

If new arrivals don't sell well within a few weeks, they are sent back to the publisher who may wholesale them out to remainderers, or pulp them.

*Self-publishers* with a professional, well-written book may have better luck with independent retailers, and not just bookshops, although they would be your first port of call. If your book has a historical or local theme, shops attached to visitor attractions here may be happy to sell it; visitors may just make that impulse buy!

Similarly, shops, bars or cafés popular with local residents are other potential outlets. If you have strong links with your home town, try an independent bookshop, garden centre or National Trust shop nearby.

You can sell at events – fêtes, fairs, markets, conferences (if you are a speaker) – or at a coffee morning, or when you give a talk to a local group.

**Be prepared!**

Keep an information sheet with you at all times with the following details: book title, author name, a one-liner with the crux of the book's plot, a paragraph expanding that (maximum 10 lines), mentioning the chief character and their dilemma, a second paragraph about you, ISBN number and how to order.

A photo of you and an image of the bookjacket add significantly, as does the whole printed in colour. And proof read it ten times; a mistake on your information sheet will destroy your credibility. Approaching any retail outlet with this sheet in your hand will immediately make you look more professional.

Always have a copy of your book with you, in the car or your bag, and take every opportunity to chat to people about it. You could have an instant sale! Obviously, you should be a little subtle in the way you go about it; nobody likes having a stranger shove a book aggressively under their nose. Selling a book personally is very rewarding; the buyer may then do you the best favour by recommending it to someone else.

And don't forget to have some bookmarks and cards made up to give to potential readers. People do tend to keep a colourful printed item when they might loose a note of your website that they scribbled down at the end of their shopping list

Consider showcasing your book on your website or blog. You don't have to set up a full e-commerce website; use a link to a payment service like PayPal which also processes credit cards. And do remember to provide a hyperlink to online retailers, such as Amazon, Waterstones Online, the Book Depository, Barnes & Noble or to independent bookshops which readers can find via the Booksellers Association (https://www.booksellers.org.uk/bookshopsearch).

## 33

## SELLING YOUR BOOK – THE EBOOK VERSION

If you are published traditionally, i.e. represented by an agent and/or with a publishing contract with a mainstream house like Orion, Penguin Random House, Harper Collins, Transworld, etc. then marketing and selling your ebook will take place alongside the printed version as I described in the last chapter. But it won't necessarily be for very long.

If you are published in ebook by one of the smaller digital-only presses, you will get some online marketing and sales support – check this in the contract. If you self-publish you are definitely the one who does the work!

Whatever your route and initial support, you need to plan your own PR and marketing strategy; your ebook will be up against the 200,000+ mainstream titles published in the UK alone each year, let alone the world. And the tens/hundreds of thousands of independently/self-published titles are additional to the 'official' listings like Nielsens.

### There is no magic formula

Selling the fruits of your hard work involves more hard work and time, but here are a few basics:

- A thoroughly edited, well-formatted ebook with a professional cover is vital
- Upload your ebook to as many platforms as possible; Amazon is the 'big beast', but don't neglect the others. You may choose to self-publish via an aggregator like Smashwords (http://www.smashwords.com) or Draft to Digital (https://www.draft2digital.com). They will convert and distribute your book for you to a range of platforms apart from Amazon Kindle
- On Amazon, apply to Author Central to set up an Author Page on each store (US, UK, DE, FR and so on). It's really easy to complete and enhances your online profile
- Get anybody you know to read your book and post an **honest** review on Amazon; potential buyers are more willing to buy books other people like. If you can get an established author or specialist in your field to write one, that will give a tremendous boost
- Look online for book review/book bloggers and approach them for a review or guest spot

**Social media**

If you are publishing in the 'digiverse', you should make yourself known there. 'Building your platform', i.e. having your website up and running before you publish your book will establish you in the eyes of potential readers. Pre-publication, you are aiming to build trust and interest about the subject area of your book.

- A website or blog (or both) with background information and, after publication, buying links; you

should aim to contribute new content at least weekly on a blog and refresh the website regularly
- A Twitter account, but use it to socialise and build up your personality; only 10% of your tweets should be 'buy my book!'
- A Facebook page which is an add-on to your normal Facebook personal profile. Here you can build up a following by posting content about your writing, books, the background to your book, etc.
- Instagram account, but like Twitter, keep it social and post 'life' photos (cats, dogs, local views, holiday photos, fun things) in between the book posts
- Contribute to other blogs: making comments, offering to write articles (posts) on their blog, having other people as guests on yours
- Support other writers and their activities; you won't lose out by giving and you will gain some good digital friends who will support you in turn
- Be authentic – a phoney can be spotted very quickly
- BE WARNED - remember that everything you put on social media is **public**, whether on a personal profile, an author page or in a group. That picture of you falling off a donkey with a glass in your hand on holiday may be hilarious, but isn't one that will enhance your writing image

These are some of the basics. However, you should not overburden yourself or do anything you truly hate. Choose the social media you enjoy doing and focus on those methods. We all have a preferred method and they are not necessarily the most effective for book sales.

For instance, I love Twitter most, but I know Facebook is more effective, so I keep a strong presence there. I'm also aware that any of these could pull the plug at any time, so I try to keep my newsletter and two blogs active and regular.

But things change fast in the book world and even faster online. Do keep looking online for further tips and hints as trends change. And good luck!

## 34

# HOW TO LAUNCH YOUR BOOK

In the last two articles, I outlined some ideas for selling your book, both print and ebooks. But the milestone event is your book launch, especially if it's your first. "But I'm not famous", "It's only my little family memoir" or "Nobody will want to buy it" are some excuses I've heard for not having a launch. The newest one is "It's only an ebook". Sorry, not good enough.

You've slaved away, often over years, dedicating all your spare hours, thinking about the book when not writing it and you've finally got there – your first book. Of course, you need to celebrate!

A launch doesn't have to be a Foyles Literary Lunch, nor does it have to be in a bookshop, nor need hundreds of attendees. It can be a bookshop event or a simple drinks evening at home with a few informal words and a nod to a pile of your books.

### Practicalities

Make sure you line up a friend who can take the cash. A writer friend of mine booked a double table at his local pub, invited a few friends and ended up speaking to the whole pub and selling over a hundred books. Plus it was reported in the local paper which prompted more sales.

Other possibilities, especially if your book relates to the place, are tourist bookshops, hotels, boats, club venue, museum, a friend's garden, art gallery, community centre – in short, anywhere where potential buyers might gather.

Refreshments? Soft drinks or tea/coffee should be laid on, but most launches feature wine or fizz. We're lucky being near the Loire Valley with both on tap. Crisps and nuts (or trays of *hors d'oeuvres* if you can run to that) are always welcome.

### So what happens at a launch?

Some are like standard parties – milling, lurking, laughing, but centred around the author and the book. The emphasis is on celebration and relaxation. A five to ten minute pause will allow the author to thank everybody, and the publisher and agent (if they have one) to say a few words. Then attendees can buy copies and queue for the author to sign them.

A more structured launch, sometimes called 'An evening with (name of author)' is ticketed – usually at a modest amount redeemable against the purchase of the book. Attendees are offered a glass of wine, fizz or soft drink on arrival. After five or ten minutes' mingling, they sit down to listen to the author give a talk for 25-30 minutes which will probably include an excerpt or two from their book. A question and answer session follows, then buying and signing and a little more mingling.

### But what if I publish ebook only?

If you possibly can, I recommend having some books printed even if it's just for the launch event and the first few months.

Both types of launch described above can be adapted, but make sure you have something for people to take away with them such as bookmarks with buying links. If you print them with uncoated paper on the reverse, you can sign the back.

**Photos, please!**

And, finally, get somebody else to take plenty of photographs especially of you holding your book, or high resolution printed image if an ebook. You can then use these photos to publicise your book further.

## 35
# HOW TO SELL MORE BOOKS – WRITE MORE BOOKS!

Agatha Christie's bestseller status is no mystery: she wrote lots and lots of books. Any writer increases their chance of becoming a bestselling author – and, just as importantly, a regular seller – just by writing more books.

Of course, we all know writers who have achieved literary immortality with a single novel, for example, Emily Brontë with *Wuthering Heights,* Harper Lee and *To Kill A Mockingbird* and Margaret Mitchell with *Gone with the Wind,* but it's much easier to name bestselling authors who have written multiple books:

- Agatha Christie – 82 (+6 as Mary Westmacott + 19 plays)
- Barbara Cartland – 723
- John Creasey – 600
- Danielle Steele – 179
- Stephen King– 70
- Georges Simenon – 570
- Nora Roberts – 200+
- Enid Blyton – 800
- James Patterson – 98

- Gilbert Patten – 209
- Penny Jordan – 200+

http://en.wikipedia.org/wiki/List_of_best-selling_fiction_authors

With just 15 books to her name, J K Rowling, who we tend to think of as being an all-time, record-breaking phenomenon, has sold only 500 million books, a fraction of the more productive Agatha Christie's total sales of 4 billion. Danielle Steele comes in at 800 million.

## Just a numbers game?

Quantity alone is not enough. A writer who follows up a successful novel with regular new books of similar (or improved!) quality will gain more sales. Of course, these books will also need active promotion. But any book following a successful predecessor will have a greater chance of success as the author will already be known to a base of fans.

It's never been easier to promote your books effectively than in the digital age. Whenever you publish a new book, you can access social media and be stocked in online bookshops for next to no cost, other than time and effort – advantages never enjoyed by earlier writers.

Four top tips for boosting serial sales available to all published writers:

- At the end of each book, add the first chapter of the next one in the series, with the planned publication date, to whet the reader's appetite and prime them to buy it as soon as it comes out.
- Create your own mailing list of fans by embedding a sign-up form on your author website which links to

a mailing list programme like MailChimp, MailerLite, AWeber, etc. so that you'll be able to contact fans and readers directly as soon as the next book is published.
- Stay in regular communication with the reading world by having either or both Goodreads and Facebook author pages and/or writing regular blogposts.
- Offer a free download of the first book in a series to hook new readers. If they enjoy it enough, they'll buy the rest of the series.
- Alternatively, if you have an established series, offer a package of short stories and a reading guide (Example here: https://alison-morton.com/newsletter/

**How to write more books**

The key is discipline. Not the *Fifty Shades of Grey* type, but sitting down, despite household and life trivia and writing. Some writers tap at their keyboards for a given time, some have a daily word target. It has to become part of your everyday routine, even if it's a snatched hour or thirty minutes at the beginning or end of the working day.

# FURTHER READING

**A selection of books I've found helpful...**

*Write to be Published*, Nicola Morgan, Snowbooks, 2011
*Love Writing*, Sue Moorcroft, Accent Press, 2010
*Self Editing for Fiction Writers*, Renni Browne & Dave King, Collins, 2nd ed., 2004
*Bestseller*, Celia Brayfield, Fourth Estate, 1996
*Wannabe a Writer We've Heard Of?*, Jane Wenham-Jones, Accent Press, 2012
*The Naked Author - a Guide to Self-Publishing,* Alison Baverstock, A & C Black Publishers Ltd; 2011
*The Seven Key Elements of Fiction*, L P Wilbur, Hale, 2001
*The 38 Most Common Writing Mistakes*, Jack M Bickham, Writer's Digest Books, 1997
*On Writing,* Stephen King, NEL, 2001
*Hooked,* Les Edgerton, Writer's Digest Books, 2007
*Finding Your Voice*, Les Edgerton, Writer's Digest Books, 2003
*From Pitch to Publication*, Carole Blake, Macmillan, 1999
*The Insider's Guide To Getting Your Book Published*, Rachael Stock, White Ladder Press, 2005
*Write a Great Synopsis*, Nicola Morgan, Crabbit Publishing, 2012

*Self-Printed: The Sane Person's Guide to Self-Publishing*, Catherine Ryan Howard, Amazon Media EU S.à r.l., 2011
*Sell Your Books!: A Book Promotion Handbook for the Self-published or Indie Author*, Debbie Young, SilverWood Books, 2012
*How to Market A Book*, Joanna Penn, 2013
*The Emotion Thesaurus*, Angela Ackerman & Becca Puglisi, 2012

**Reference**
*Roget's Thesaurus*, ed. George Davidson, Penguin, 2002
*Grammar Girl's Quick and Dirty Tips for Better Writing*, Mignon Fogarty, St Martin's Press, 2008
*Complete Plain Words*, HMSO (after Gowers) Penguin, 1986
*Elements of Style*, Strunk & White, Pearson Longman, 2009
*Writers' & Artists' Yearbook*, Alysoun Owen, ed. Bloomsbury

# SOME USEFUL WEB AND BLOGSITES

**Writers' organisations**
The Society of Authors https://www.societyofauthors.org
The Romantic Novelists' Association https://www.rna-uk.org/
The Historical Novel Society https://historicalnovelsociety.org
The Crime Writers' Association https://thecwa.co.uk
The Alliance of Independent Authors https://allianceindependentauthors.org
Women Writers http://booksbywomen.org/

**Courses**
Arvon Foundation https://www.arvon.org

**Publishing**
Writers & Artists Yearbook https://www.writersandartists.co.uk
The Independent Publishing magazine online http://www.theindependentpublishingmagazine.com
List of small publishers https://www.ipgbook.com/publishers-pages-32.php
Apple (iBooks) https://itunespartner.apple.com/books/

Amazon self-publishing (KDP) https://kdp.amazon.com
IngramSpark https://www.ingramspark.com
Draft2Digital https://www.draft2digital.com
Smashwords http://www.smashwords.com
Kobo Writing Life https://www.kobo.com/us/en/p/writinglife
Barnes & Noble/Nook https://press.barnesandnoble.com/

**Social media**
Facebook www.facebook.com
Twitter www.twitter.com
Instagram https://www.instagram.com
Blogger www.blogger.com
Wordpress www.wordpress.com

**Other**
WritersOnline (Writing Magazine) https://www.writers-online.co.uk

## WOULD YOU LEAVE A REVIEW?

I hope you enjoyed *The 500 Word Writing Buddy* and found the information useful.

If you did, I'd really appreciate it if you would write a few words of review on the site where you purchased this book.

Reviews help books to feature more prominently on retailer sites and help more people on their writing journey.

Very many thanks!

# THE ROMA NOVA THRILLER SERIES

*The Carina Mitela adventures*

### INCEPTIO

Early 21st century. Terrified after a kidnap attempt, New Yorker Karen Brown, has a harsh choice – being terminated by government enforcer Renschman or fleeing to Roma Nova, her dead mother's homeland in Europe.

Founded sixteen hundred years ago by Roman exiles and ruled by women, it gives Karen safety, at a price. But Renschman follows and sets a trap she has no option but to enter.

### CARINA – *A novella*

Carina Mitela is still an inexperienced officer in the Praetorian Guard Special Forces of Roma Nova. Disgraced for a disciplinary offence, she is sent out of everybody's way to bring back a traitor from the Republic of Quebec. But when she discovers a conspiracy reaching into the highest levels of Roma Nova, what price is personal danger against fulfilling the mission?

### PERFIDITAS

Falsely accused of conspiracy, 21$^{st}$ century Praetorian Carina Mitela flees into the criminal underworld. Hunted by the security services and traitors alike, she struggles to save her beloved Roma Nova as well as her own life. Who is her ally and who her enemy? But the ultimate betrayal is waiting for her…

### SUCCESSIO

21$^{st}$ century Praetorian Carina Mitela's attempt to resolve a past family indiscretion is spiralling into a nightmare. Convinced her beloved husband has deserted her, and with her enemy holding a gun to the imperial heir's head, Carina has to make the hardest decision of her life.

*The Aurelia Mitela adventures*

## AURELIA

Late 1960s. Sent to Berlin to investigate silver smuggling, former Praetorian Aurelia Mitela barely escapes a near-lethal trap. Her old enemy is at the heart of all her troubles and she pursues him back home to Roma Nova but he strikes at her most vulnerable point – her young daughter.

## NEXUS – *A novella*

Mid 1970s. Aurelia Mitela is serving as Roma Nova's interim ambassador in London. Asked by a British colleague to find his missing son, Aurelia is sure he'll turn up only a little worse for wear.

But a spate of high-level killings pulls Aurelia away into a dangerous pan-European investigation and the killers threaten to terminate her life companion.

But Aurelia is a Roma Novan – they never give up…

## INSURRECTIO

Early 1980s. Caius Tellus, the charismatic leader of a rising nationalist movement, threatens to destroy Roma Nova.

Aurelia Mitela, ex-Praetorian and imperial councillor, attempts to counter the growing fear and instability. But it may be too late to save Roma Nova from meltdown and herself from destruction by her lifelong enemy….

## RETALIO

Early 1980s Vienna. Aurelia Mitela chafes at her enforced exile. She barely escaped from her nemesis, Caius Tellus, who has grabbed power in Roma Nova.

Aurelia is determined to liberate her homeland. But Caius's manipulations have ensured that she is ostracised by her fellow exiles.

Powerless and vulnerable, Aurelia fears she will never see Roma Nova again.

## ROMA NOVA EXTRA

*A collection of short stories*

*Four historical and four present day and a little beyond*

A young tribune sent to a backwater in 370 AD for practising the wrong religion, his lonely sixty-fifth descendant labours in the 1980s to reconstruct her country. A Roma Novan imperial councillor attempting to stop the Norman invasion of England in 1066, her 21st century Praetorian descendant flounders as she searches for her own happiness.

Some are love stories, some are lessons learned, some resolve tensions and unrealistic visions, some are plain adventures, but above all, they are stories of people in dilemmas and conflict, and their courage and effort to resolve them.

---

**Military or civilians?**

**The curious anomaly of the German Women's Auxiliary Services during the Second World War**

Nearly 500,000 young German women served in uniform with the German armed forces in the Second World War yet their history is rarely recalled in Germany and is virtually unknown in the Anglophone world. A unique study, in English, of the lives and work of this forgotten female army.

www.ingramcontent.com/pod-product-compliance
Lightning Source LLC
LaVergne TN
LVHW012025060526
838201LV00061B/4465